Deep Apple Pie
Language and the Law in Canada

Keyvan Sayar

Keyvan Sayar, M.A., LL.M., studied law and political science at Université Paris Ouest, Sciences Po Grenoble and Trinity College Dublin. He worked for seven years in the NGO sector before joining the French ministry of foreign affairs. He is also a fiction writer.

www.keyvansayar.com

Published by ZOON POLITIKON

and printed by Books In Print®

©Keyvan Sayar 2006

ISBN-13: 978-1493792191

ISBN-10: 1493792199

The advantages of living

with two cultures

Strike one at every turn,

Especially when one finds a notice

in an office building:

"This elevator will not run

on Ascension Day";

Or reads in the *Montreal Star*:

"Tomorrow being the Feast

of the Immaculate Conception,

There will be no collection

of garbage in the city";

Or sees on the restaurant menu

the bilingual dish:

DEEP APPLE PIE

TARTE AUX POMMES PROFONDES[1]

F.R. Scott [2]

---

[1] Literally : *Pie with deep apples*

[2] in *The Blasted Pine,* Macmillan (Toronto), 1957 – Francis Reginald Scott (1899-1985) was a Canadian jurist and poet.

TABLE OF CONTENTS

INTRODUCTION 11

   I. PRELIMINARY CONSIDERATIONS ON LANGUAGE 19

      A. Language as a mirror of the mind............19

      B. Law v. Droit and Loi...................................23

   II. ELEMENTS ON THE HISTORY OF CANADA 27

        1. The Aboriginals 27

        2. The discovery of Canada..............................28

        3. The rise and fall of New France 29

        4. The British North America (B.N.A.)..............31

        5. The repatriation of the Canadian

Constitution..33

   III. THE ENCOUNTER OF THE CIVIL LAW AND THE COMMON

LAW 35

        1. The main features of the civil law 37

           a) Clear and comprehensive codes 38

           b) Substantive law and the notion of rights

....47

           c) The limited powers of the judiciary 50

        2. The main features of the Common Law 54

           a) A legal patchwork....................................56

           b) A powerful and independent Judiciary..67

               (1) The birth of the English Judiciary 67

               (2) The judges' independence 69

(3) The principle of *stare decisis* 71
c) A pragmatic and concrete law 75
(1) The communal character of the common law 75
(2) The forms of action: the writs 77
3. The Canadian mix 79
(1) New France's legacy in Québec 80
aa) French customary law 80
bb) The roots of bilingualism in Québec: "Speak French and we shall obey" ... 84
cc) The mix of old French law and English law 89
(2) The continuity of French and English influences in Québec 96
aa) The extra-territorial sources of law 97
bb) Continuity and identity in Québec's new Civil Code 105
(3) The United States' influence 109
(4) The lost Aboriginal legacy 114
(5) Towards a bijural legal education in Canada 116

IV. LANGUAGE LAWS IN CANADA: FROM TOLERANCE TO RECOGNITION 121
1. A first step towards official bilingualism: the British North America Act (1867) 122
2. Manitoba: from bilingualism to unilingualism (1870 – 1989) 126

3. Northwest Territories, Alberta, Saskatchewan: the forgotten bilingualism (1870 – 1989) 129
    a) The Northwest Territories 129
    b) Alberta and Saskatchewan 133
4. Québec's Quiet Revolution (1960s) 135
5. The Royal Commission on Bilingualism and Biculturalism (1963-69) 141
6. The Official Languages Act: official bilingualism becomes a reality in practice (1969) 148
7. Resistance in Québec: the Charter of the French Language (1977) 152
8. The Canadian Charter of Rights and Freedoms (1982) 157
9. The Second Official Languages Act (1988) 158
    a) A bigger role for the Commissioner of Official Languages 159
    b) Entrenchment of bilingualism in the National Capital Region 164
10. The incomplete recognition of Aboriginal peoples' rights 168
    a) A special status for Aboriginals 168
    b) The absence of language rights 175

V. LEGISLATION AND LANGUAGE 183
1. General considerations on bilingual legislation 183
    a) The question of draftsmanship 184
        (1) Unilingual drafting and translation 186
            aa) Subsequent translation 186

- bb) Participatory translation 193
- (2) Bilingual drafting 195
- aa) Co-drafting...............................196
- bb) Double drafting 197
- b) The question of phrasing 199
- (1) Steering clear from le double entendre 201
- (2) Adopting a simple style 211
- c) The material constraints.......................216
- 2. The Federal legislature 219
- 3. Provincial legislatures.................................227
- 4. Subordinate legislation...............................229

VI. THE CANADIAN JUDICIARY AND LANGUAGE............235

- 1. Courts of first instance 238
- a) Provincial courts...................................238
- (1) The right to an interpreter 241
- (2) The case of Quebec 244
- (3) The case of New Brunswick...........248
- (4) The case of Nunavut......................253
- b) Federal courts 261
- 2. The Supreme Court.....................................268
- a) The creation of the Supreme Court 268
- (1) A general court of appeal for Canada 268
- (2) The extension of the Court's jurisdiction 274
- aa) A general jurisdiction...............274
- bb) The independence from the Privy Council...275

cc) The Court and the Constitution 277
b) Bilingualism at the Supreme Court 279
(1) Language(s) of work 279
aa) 1875 – 1969: An English-speaking Supreme Court 282
bb) 1970 – 1980: The first Official Languages Act..286
cc) 1980 – 1988: An English-based bilingualism 289
dd) 1988 – today: The second Official Languages Act..292
(2) The equal authenticity rule and its implications...294
(3) The method of interpretation of statutes 298
aa) Interpreting each version of a statute in the light of the other.....................298
bb) Looking into the genesis of each piece of legislation 301
cc) Protecting the interests of the people..304
(4) Interpretation of two versions of a court judgment 305
CONCLUSION 309

BIBLIOGRAPHY **313**

ANNEXES **326**

INTRODUCTION

According to Canadian poet Frank Oliver Call, *"the soul of Canada is a dual personality, and must remain only half revealed to those who know only one language"*[3]. With each of Canada's official languages comes indeed a mindset, a culture, a legacy.

In the legal field, much has been written about Quebec's mixed jurisdiction and the influence of the United States on Canadian law. The Canadian legal system is indeed quite a mix. Bijuralism in Quebec, the federal / provincial division of powers, Nunavut's one-of-a-kind Aboriginal legal order and the influence of the United States are all

---

[3] Frank Oliver Call, *The Spell of French Canada*

elements of that clearly distinguish Canada from Great Britain (its 'mother country').

But the legacy of the civil law tradition and the particularities of the common law do not suffice to characterize its legal system. Language, an often overlooked element, has come to play a key role in Canadian law. The country has indeed developed, over the past two centuries (and especially over the past decades), a unique bilingual legal culture.

Bilingualism is not a double unilingualism. Canadian history has been marked by the confrontation of the French and British nationalisms. The way to social peace was official bilingualism (and as far as Quebec was concerned, official bijuralism[4]).

---

[4] As will be explained later, at the very beginning of the British rule, French Canadians were granted the right to

There were several major steps in this direction, especially in the 1960s and 1970s, where the federal government promoted effective official bilingualism to counter the movement for the independence of Quebec.

Making laws in two languages implies specific drafting considerations. In a context where two versions of one law are both equally authoritative, if one version is not as clear as the other one, it is not just language equality that is endangered, it is the very principle of legality[5].

---

continue to use their language and their laws.

[5] As will be explained later, in the early years of Canadian bilingualism, many statutes were drafted in English and poorly translated in French, which constituted in an impediment to fully understand the law for French-speakers.

Administering justice in two languages and interpreting two versions of the law to issue judgments also implies specific techniques. The Canadian Supreme Court has come up with its very own way to interpret the law, treating the two versions as two inseparable components of one same norm. The problem posed by this method is that only people with a good command of both official languages can understand the law. The poet was right, the soul of Canada remains only half revealed to those who only speak one of its languages (which is the case for 85% of the Canadian population).

Legal comparatist Esin Orücü proposed a colourful system of classification for mixed jurisdictions. Using culinary metaphors she created several categories, ranging from purée (thorough blend of systems) to mixing bowl (ingredients in the process of being blended), Italian style salad (distinct but intermingled ingredients covered by dressing) and salad plate (ingredients sitting separately on a flat plate)[6]. One could hardly deny her statement that *"all legal systems are the outcome of mixtures"*[7], yet one could legitimately wonder at what stage a legal system starts to be considered a mixed jurisdiction and if – once it has been thus labelled - it can ever come out of this category.

According to most legal comparatists' criteria, Canada is not as such a mixed jurisdiction. Its system is usually classified in the common law tradition. Yet, bilingualism

---

[6] Esin Örücü, *Mixed and mixing systems : a conceptual search,* p. 344, in E. Örücü, *Studies in Legal Systems : "Mixed and Mixing",* Kluwer Law International, 1996, 384 p.

[7] *Ibid.* p. 342

distinguishes it from its legal matrix (Britain) and its influential neighbour (the United States). Canada's legal system does not seem to correspond to any of the Orücü's categories. But could it not have become a *sui generis* jurisdiction, where common lawyers have been influenced by civil law and civilians by common law? A country where the linguistic question has resulted in a new unique bilingual way to deal with the law? A jurisdiction where legal legacies combined with bilingualism would have brought about a new recipe, perhaps that of the ambiguous deep apple pie / tarte aux pommes profondes?

After preliminary considerations on the impact of language on the law (I), Canada's dual context - its history, its legal system - will be examined (II). The establishment of effective official bilingualism in Canada as well as its consequences on legislation and the judiciary will then be considered (III).

18

I. PRELIMINARY CONSIDERATIONS ON LANGUAGE

A. Language as a mirror of the mind

For German philosopher Gottfried Wilhelm von Leibniz, language is a mirror of the mind that reflects into the mind and from there into concepts of order. The mind, the approach of people would thus result in rules and laws.

More generally American linguist Benjamin Lee Whorf thought that language and signs in general shape the world into a topiary garden.

In the Whorfian theory of linguistic relativity, in addition to being a communication instrument, language molds ideas and programs mental activity. Thus people with different native languages would not have the same view of the universe or might find it difficult to communicate on certain topics.

There is only one word for snow in English while there are several in Inuit. The Inuit speaker is required to note distinctions (e.g. whether the snow is on the ground or falling) but the English speaker only needs to note the distinctions if the occasion arises.

It is difficult to determine whether what we say is what we see or what we see is what we say. Generations of linguists have argued over this question. Whorf's theory has been criticized, but the idea that a language has its own concepts and thus tends to have an influence on the way one sees the world is accepted by most linguists. This is what interests us here.

For legal comparatist Bernhard Grossfeld, the often overlooked role of language in the law is central:

"(L)anguages are not neutral. They operate powerfully out of often unconscious backgrounds and they reduce a complex reality to make it manageable in our own contexts and in the directions which we prefer. This raises doubts about whether a language can fit into another background – not necessarily because of the differences in the nature of human beings but because of differences in the way human beings choose and rely on words"[8]

In most monolingual jurisdictions, the question of language can only been studied in

---

[8] Bernhard Grossfeld, *Comparatists and Languages* in *Comparative legal studies: Traditions and Transitions*, Cambridge University Press, 2003, 520 p., p. 157

regard to semantic evolution or style in the expression. This is in itself a vast and fascinating field of study.

In jurisdictions that use several languages other issues become important too. Expressing the same idea in two or more languages is quite a challenge. Making a justice system (and also a government, a state administration) work smoothly in several languages, without giving prominence to one of the languages is perhaps an even bigger challenge. These questions are becoming relevant for more and more jurisdictions as countries become part of regional unions and international organisations.

B. Law v. *Droit* and *Loi*

Without even going into the French approach to law-making and justice (which will be examined later), one can note a semantic gap between English and French definitions of the word "Law".

In French, "Law" is translated as *Droit* (which means Right) or as *Loi* (which means Statute). While *Droit* has a clearly political connotation (law as a set of fundamental rules and rights), *Loi* refers to the legislative power (law as a statute made by the authorities). There is no rule of precedent in the French legal system and the type of law made by courts, known in English as case-law is translated into *Jurisprudence*. In English there is a semantic connection between the two concepts (united in the word "case"-"law"), in French there is none. Someone trained in

French law will therefore be able to conceive the general legal implications of an important court decision but will not put it in the same general category (of *Droit* or *Loi*) as a new statute passed by the parliament. Statute-law and case-law are not related. In the French civilian perspective, statutes are the law and judgements are merely jurisprudence, i.e. the expression of opinions in cases where the statutes did not give sufficiently clear directions.

One manifestation of the English influence on the legal profession in French-speaking Canada is the use of the terms *Droit jurisprudentiel* to refer to case-law. These terms, rarely used in the French context (except by researchers in comparative law, legal history or legal sociology) are commonly used in Canada. There the concept of law (and legal principles) has been reconciled with the notion of court decision. When new concepts come in a culture, new words are created.

II. ELEMENTS ON THE HISTORY OF CANADA

The scope of this dissertation does not allow a long and thorough presentation of Canadian history. This object of this part is rather to present a concise overview of Canadian history.

1. The Aboriginals

Although most history books see the "discovery" of Canada the starting point of the country's history, it is important to mention that Aboriginal nations have been living on the territory for over 4,000 years.

2. The discovery of Canada

The first Europeans to come to Canada were Vikings from Iceland and Greenland in the 10th century[9]. But their journeys to Canada ceased and the depictions of these distant shores became myths.

---

[9] Contrary to what is often believed, the first Europeans to settle in Canada were neither French nor English. They were Vikings from Iceland and Greenland. They apparently visited the North-eastern coast of Canada. In AD 986, Viking sailor Bjarni Herjólfsson was driven to Canada by a storm. Icelandic navigator Leif Eriksson sailed by the coasts of Labrador and Newfoundland. During his voyage, he found an area where plenty of grapes were growing which he called Vinland. The location of Vinland is not clearly established but historians think it was in L'Anse aux Meadows in Northern Newfoundland. The remains of a Viking village were found there in the 1960s. The contact between the Vikings and the Amerindians seems to have been conflictual but there is also some evidence of trading exchanges.

Canada was re-discovered by sailors in the 15th century. They established several fisheries in Newfoundland. Jacques Cartier sailed down the Saint Lawrence river in 1535 and claimed the lands for France, while England claimed the southern part of Newfoundland in 1583. English and French settlements in North America started in the 1600s.

3. The rise and fall of New France

The first lasting French settlement in Canada was that of Quebec (established in 1608) by the Saint Lawrence river. Over the next 150 years, more French settlements were set up in the Saint Lawrence region.

In 1627, the French government entrusted the *Compagnie des Cent-Associés* with the mission of establishing a French empire in North America. The *Compagnie* did not manage to achieve this aim, and its charter was withdrawn in 1663. King Louis XIV thus took possession of New France. In 1664, his Minister Colbert formed the Company of West Indies which was granted the monopoly of fur trade. Through the company's Charter, he introduced the Custom of Paris as the body of law governing New France[10].

But one century later, the French colonies of Canada were taken over by the British after the costly and painful French and Indian war. The French Canadians from Acadia were deported and the ones from Quebec

---

[10] For the King, order was essential to the expansion of the colony, a Sovereign Council was therefore established at Quebec. It acted as a court of appeal from courts of first instance in civil and criminal matters.

became subjects of the British King. In 1763, France formally conceded its Canadian territories to Britain in the *Treaty of Paris*. The treaty tolerated the French Canadians' Roman Catholic faith.

4. The British North America (B.N.A.)

The British North America originally comprised territories in what are now the United States and Canada. It was greatly reduced with the American revolution.

In 1774, for fear that the French Canadians would side with the American rebel colonies, the British authorities granted them the right to use their law and their language[11].

---

[11] In the *Quebec Act*. – There were nonetheless rebellions against the British government in the following

After having pacified their relations, the U.S.A. and the British government agreed on a border separating the U.S.A. from the B.N.A.[12] in the west.

Agitation for a confederation of the colonies grew in the first half of the 19th century. A first *Act of Union* united Ontario (Upper Canada) and Quebec (Lower Canada) in 1840. In 1867, a confederation was created by the *British North America Act*. The act granted this new Canadian confederation an autonomous status[13], its own parliament, government and general court of appeal.

5. The repatriation of the Canadian Constitution

---

century (in 1837-1838).

[12] This border was the 49th parallel north.

[13] Canada became a British dominion.

Canada went through most the 19th and 20th centuries as a British dominion. But as a national identity developed, Canadian politicians sought to gain more independence from Westminster. The 1931 Statute of Westminster granted Canada equality with the United Kingdom within the British Empire. In 1949, the Canadian Supreme Court became the country's court of last resort[14]. In 1982, the Canadian Constitution was repatriated, thus severing the last remaining link of subordination to the Parliament of the United Kingdom. Canada is now fully independent.

---

[14] As will be explained later, until 1949 the Judicial Committee of the Privy Council in England was hearing appeals from Canada in last resort.

III. THE ENCOUNTER OF THE CIVIL LAW AND THE COMMON LAW

Canada and the province of Québec are cited in numerous works of comparative law as a good example of mixed jurisdiction, an encounter between the civil law and common law traditions. The province of Québec (formerly referred to as Canada or Lower Canada) was indeed originally a French colony. When it was taken over by Britain, its people were subjected to the English crown but were authorized to keep their old laws and use their language. As will be explained later[15], French was subsequently recognized as an official language in all of Canada, thus furthering the mixing of the jurisdiction.

---

[15] See the part on Language laws in Canada.

It has created a unique legal order which apart from England and France has also been strongly influenced by Canada's mighty neighbour.

The main features of the civil law will be examined now. It is important to mention that some of these features were not very developed at the time French Canada became British. They are yet of interest here because French-speaking Canada and France maintained an active dialogue under the British rule. While several features of the French civilian tradition were brought to Canada by French settlers, several others came later, through the books.

1. The main features of the civil law

The Civil law tradition is hard to define or label. While historians trace it back to the Roman Empire this tradition has undergone many changes through the years and has been adapted to dozens of different contexts (in space and in time). The law of Emperor Justinian's days and that of contemporary France seem indeed to have as many differences as they have commonalities[16].

---

[16] As Pr. H. P. Glenn noted : *"There are leading characteristics today of a Civil Law tradition – codification is the most obvious of them – but these are present characteristics, and we cannot cast them backwards as having always constituted the leading version of the tradition. There have been too many stops and starts, too many reversals and recommencements, to conclude as to a constant tradition. This tells us already something about change in continental law. Maybe change is the tradition"*. See p.117 of H. Patrick Glenn, *Legal Traditions of the World*,

Since the law evolves with the needs, practices and mores of a society, it is constantly subject to change. As long as a legal tradition is not extinct, one could hardly give a definitive description of what it consists in. The aim of this section will therefore not be to define Civil Law but rather to see what the main features of this legal tradition are.

a) Clear and comprehensive codes

The Civil law tradition owes its fame and arguably its name to Emperor Justinian's Corpus of Civil Law (*Corpus Iuris Civilis*). This *Corpus* was a compilation of the main laws of Rome and citations of the main authoritative jurists on various issues[17] within a few volumes.

O.U.P., 2000, 371 p.

Roman law was already developed, complex and admired long before Justinian, but the work of compilation and simplification ordered by the Emperor constituted a turning point in legal history. Justinian's corpus was the first elaborate, comprehensive and ready-to-use legal tool.

Redaction of the law facilitated the establishment of a more uniform legal education and practice throughout the empire. This was maybe one of the main characteristics of the Civil Law at that time: in a few books, the *Corpus* covered all imaginable legal topics, providing clear

[17] The Corpus Iuris Civilis contained : the Institutes (an elementary textbook for students of law), the Digest (a compilation of edited juristic writings), the Codex (a collection of imperial enactments) and the Novels (Justinian's own enactments subsequent to the publication of the three other parts). See p. 3, O.F. Robinson, T.D. Fergus, W.M. Gordon, *European Legal History*, 3rd Edition, Butterworths, 2000, 385 p.

procedures and solutions. In a context where laws were different from village to village, the Roman Civil Law's thoroughness was precious. The grandeur of the Roman Empire gave it legitimacy (even in the eyes of people who were not under the empire's domination). These reasons might explain its subsequent success even after the disappearance of the Roman Empire.

The codification movement which was to occur centuries later in continental Europe (with the famous *Code Napoléon*[18]) shared these characteristics. Codification appealed to people as it provided codes covering whole fields of law comprehensively in a clear and simple language. So clear that while working

---

[18] The *Code Napoléon* was the French civil code. Six other codes covering topics such as criminal law and civil procedure were published alongside the *Code Napoléon*. It was therefore not just the civil law which was codified but virtually all of French law.

on his novel *the Charterhouse of Parma,* Stendhal would read three pages of the *Code Napoléon*[19] every day before he started writing. He affirmed that this helped him keep a *"natural"* style[20]. The codes thus made law

---

[19] The French civil code having been written under the supervision of Napoléon is often referred to as *Code Napoléon*. Napoléon did not come up with the idea of having a civil code (a civil code was already being prepared after the revolution) but it is under his rule that the first modern civil code came into being. He is said to have personally attended many preparatory meetings with the drafters in order to make sure that a layman unfamiliar with legal vocabulary (such as him) would be able to understand all the articles of the code. As mentioned above, this clarity in the phrasing of the code is often presented as one of its most important characteristics. That clarity might be due in part to Napoleon's active participation in the preparation of the code. See …

[20] Cf. Letter from Stendhal to Honoré de Balzac cited by G. de Broglie in *La Langue du Code Civil*, Académie des Sciences Morales et Politiques (http://www.asmp.fr/fiches_academiciens/textacad/broglie/code_civil.pdf).

accessible to anyone who could read and empowered all literate citizens by informing them of their rights[21].

This idea of codification as crucial to the fulfilment of the principle of legality goes back a long way. In 462 B.C. in Rome, a plebeian requested the publication of the Twelve Tables (the fundamental laws) in the form of a code. The tables were kept secret from the public yet enforced with great severity upon the plebeians[22]. This old

---

[21] As a consequence of the *"desire to overthrow legal institutions based on privilege"* there was *"a desire for law to be simplified and to be made easy to discover by any citizen who wished to know his rights and the limitations on them"*. p. 253-254, O.F. Robinson, T.D. Fergus, W.M. Gordon, *European Legal History*, 3rd Edition, Butterworths, 2000, 385 p.

[22] In his *History of Rome*, Titus Livius (a.k.a. Livy), reported that in the year 462 B.C., a plebeian named Terentilius demanded the publication of the Twelve Tables (the fundamental Roman laws) in the form of a code. These laws

example shows that behind the idea of codification there is not just that of efficiency, there is also the principle of legality (or as the Romans put it: *nulla poena sine lege*[23]).

Codification also allowed a uniform law to be applied throughout a country. Be it under Justinian's rule or in Napoleonic France. Between the fall of the Roman empire and the codification movement in Europe (starting in the 19th century), while Civil Law was still applied and used in many places[24], lots of other laws were applied.

---

which had been kept secret from the general public by the patricians were enforced with great severity upon the plebeians. Terentilius requested the publication of the tables so that plebeians would know the law. They would thus not be sentenced by surprise. – See Titus Livius, *History of Rome (Ab Urbe Condita)*, Book III Chapter 9: The Terentilian Law (see http://www.romansonline.com/sources/Hor/).

[23] Nulla poena sine lege : No penalty without a law

[24] More particularly through its religious version : the

In France, apart from some royal ordinances on precise matters, there was no uniform law throughout the country until the publication of the *Code Civil*. The aberrance of this state of things was made manifest through the writings of several French thinkers such as Blaise Pascal[25] or Voltaire[26] which stigmatized such disparities.

Catholic church's Canon Law.

[25] *"(W)e see neither justice nor injustice which does not change its nature with change in climate. Three degrees of latitude reverse all jurisprudence; a meridian decides the truth. Fundamental laws change after a few years of possession; right has its epochs; the entry of Saturn into the Lion marks to us the origin of such and such a crime. A strange justice that is bounded by a river! Truth on this side of the Pyrenees, error on the other side."*, n°294 in Blaise Pascal, *Pensées*, Gallimard, 1995 (first published in 1669), 764 p.

[26] *"Is it not an absurd and terrible thing that what is true in one village is false in another ? What kind of barbarism is it that citizens must live under different laws ?... When you travel in this kingdom you change legal systems as often as*

The *Code Civil* was published several decades after French Canada was overtaken by the British. At the time it was both an object of admiration and a heavily criticised instrument. On the one hand it was admired for its clarity and rationality[27]. On the other hand it was criticized because it embodied the values of the French revolution.

But codification was already developed in France prior to this. The *Code Louis*[28] and the sinister *Code Noir*[29] are good examples of

---

you change horses", Voltaire cited by K. Zweigert and H. Kötz at p. 80 in *An Introduction to Comparative Law*, O.U.P., 1998, 714 p.

[27] The merits of codification were voiced in the English-speaking world by English philosopher Jeremy Bentham. Bentham did not manage to get English law codified but his opinions were quite influential in the long run.

[28] The *Code Louis* was issued in 1667

[29] The *Code Noir* (Black Code) was issued in 1685 in Versailles by French King Louis XIV. It was a codification of all French laws regarding slaves. In 1724, a stricter, less

the recourse to codification in France. These codes were used in New France. So were the customs of Paris, which were used to govern French Canada. Thus even in the fields of customs, redaction (if not codification) had already occurred, giving a permanent character and a precise expression to old traditions.

b) Substantive law and the notion of rights

The concept of rights – arguably almost nonexistent in the Common Law[30] – is another feature of the Civil Law tradition. It seems to

---

liberal version of the *Code Noir* was made for Louisiana where the white population was concerned with the increase in the number of free black people. Louisiana was at the time part of New France and under the authority of the Governor General based in Québec.

[30] See below, Chapter 1, paragraph 2.3

have been developed as an instrument in overcoming feudal hierarchy.

Long before feudalism, the Roman Civil Law was already explicit as to rights and duties. There was a law of family (covering a wide range of subjects going from adoption to divorce[31]), a law of ownership (with a complex classification comprising many categories[32]), a variety of contracts[33], sanctions against delictual conduct…

Roman Law had not been created *ex nihilo* by philosophers, priests and politicians. It had been inspired by the concrete realities

---

[31] Within Roman family law there were rights and duties, for example the right to divorce, at the initiative of the husband or the wife, see *ibid.* p. 119

[32] There were many criteria used for organising the world of things : patrimonial / extra-patrimonial things ; common / sacred things ; principal / accessorial things ; corporeal / incorporeal things…, see *ibid.* p. 120

[33] Real contracts, verbal contracts, literal contracts and consensual contracts, see *ibid.* p. 120

of Roman life and had incorporated elements of pre-Roman law[34]. At the origin, it was largely casuistic[35], but centuries of legal

---

[34] *"Just 3,000 years ago Europe was a very chthonic place. (...) The action (...) wasn't in Europe, it was further south and east. They Egyptians had already built the pyramids; Babylon was becoming one of the seven wonders of the world. (...) The Greeks must have known about these efforts, hence the great argument today about whether Greek philosophy was all Greek or whether it too built on things already known. Eventually some people in Europe, more particularly in Rome, began to think that all this fancy thinking had consequences for law (lawyers have always had to adjust their law to the societies they live in). So things began to happen in Rome which were identifiable as legal. But they didn't write a civil code; they did things very slowly (again, there is no clear line between the chthonic and the non-chthonic)."* See *ibid* p. 117

[35] *"(The) tradition of Roman law does not grow out of something called legislation, still less codification. There was occasional legislation, as there was in other communities (...) but it was for exceptional questions, of general importance. Today we would call it public law, but it was a very limited form of public law, one with little or no impact on the lives of individual people."* See *ibid.* p. 118,

decisions and the evolution of the justice system had brought about clear-cut laws on many topics.

The Romans took their law all over Europe. It was neither enforced nor accepted everywhere. After the fall of the Roman Empire, the old local laws came back to the fore in most parts of Europe.

c) The limited powers of the judiciary

Nowadays in most democratic civil law countries, the people (through their representatives) are seen as the only legitimate source of the law. Judges, being devoid of any representative mandate, are therefore not supposed to create law, but just to apply it[36].

This is rather well illustrated by the example of the French revolution. Under the *"Ancien Régime"*[37], regional *"Parlements"* (lit. Parliaments) had a wide jurisdiction which

---

[36] Some democracies (esp. American States caught between the common law tradition and the civilian influence) have circumvented this issue by having their judges elected by the people. The judges' legal and political leeway thus being legitimised by their election.

[37] The Ancien Régime (lit. : the "former regime") is a term commonly used to describe French monarchy prior to the 1789 revolution. The Ancien Régime was characterised – among other things – by a strong centralised government.

comprised the administration of justice (like a court) but also local legal production (like a parliament). *Parlements* were such a powerful counter-power that the monarchs made sure not to set up any in the new lands[38]. This institution was criticized by many (both monarchists and democrats) as an illegitimate *"gouvernement des juges"* (government of judges).

For H.P. Glenn, in Civil Law countries there is a certain form of distrust towards judges. *"Given the ancien régime, nobody wants a 'gouvernement des juges', so the primacy of the codes, and legislation in general, is reinforced by ongoing skepticism towards, and even surveillance of (through control of the career structure) the civilian judiciary"*[39].

---

[38] See below "The suppression of counter-powers"

[39] See p. 135 in H. Patrick Glenn, *Legal Traditions of the*

In post-revolutionary France, judges were seen as an arbitrary power while the statutes were perceived as an expression of the people's will. The judge's role was therefore redefined in order to make him[40] the servant of the law and not the other way round. France entered the era of the *"juge machine"* (machine judge) supposed to rely on the codes to settle the cases with a clear prohibition to put his oar in. The French *Code Civil* gave him a margin of appreciation in cases where the law would be unclear or badly drafted[41] but bound him not to make any general statement in a decision[42]. Before 1789, statutes and royal ordinances regulated society very loosely and the *Parlements* were

---

World, O.U.P., 2000, 371 p.

[40] I have allowed myself to refer to the judge as a He due to the fact that there were no female judges at that time.

[41] Article 4 of the *Code Civil*.

[42] Article 5 of the *Code Civil*.

a notable source of the law. Things changed radically after the revolution. Codes and statutes became the source of general principles while court decisions only contained specific solutions to precise problems.

The Napoleonic empire or the subsequent return of monarchy did not change this (r)evolution.

The existence of predefined rights which do not depend on judicial determination also led to a greater number of cases being brought before the courts[43]. The augmentation in lawsuits forced the judges to focus on verifying the facts and applying the

---

[43] *"It's also hard to even see the judiciary behind the mountain of cases. (...) Given a world of pre-existing rights there is no judiciary in the world which can catch up with the claims, and the backlog of cases in the civil law world rises with even more regularity than it does in the common law world."* p. 135 in H. Patrick Glenn, *Legal Traditions of the World*, O.U.P., 2000, 371 p.

provisions of the statutes rather than on creating precedents and defining new legal principles[44].

2. The main features of the Common Law

While many civil lawyers would agree with Sir Thomas Holland's definition of the Common Law as *"chaos with an index"*[45] it would be quite unfair to depict it as an incoherent legal tradition. Its complex evolution through history does not allow one to sum it up in just a few words or principles[46].

---

[44] *"If everyone has pre-defined rights (...), then their violation may exist prior to judgment, and the judicial function is largely one of verification of claims of violation of pre-existing rights, and remedying the violations." Ibid.* p. 135

[45] Quoted by H. Patrick Glenn, p.219, *ibid*.

[46] As legal comparatist H. P. Glenn noted: *"Like the ship of*

The Common Law has indeed evolved much and in diverse ways throughout the world[47]. In the past and the current century, the growth of international law has even worked to bring all legal traditions closer so that old particularities are progressively eroded in many fields[48].

---

the Argonauts rebuilt in its entirety, there are few constituent parts of the original structure still remaining. It's still the same ship and it's still the common law, but a twelfth-century English lawyer would find many surprises in the contemporary world of the common law, both in its society of origin and beyond", H. Patrick Glenn, p.221, *ibid.*

[47] *"From an Islamic or Talmudic perspective, there may appear to be schools of common law scattered about the world and, as in other complex, major traditions, some measure of internal tolerance is necessary to maintain an overarching tradition. So, as there may be Islams, so there may be common laws, though neither idea is uncontroversial."*, H.P. Glenn, p. 228, *op. cit.*

[48] In recent times *"American, English and civilian lines of legal thought have been following similar paths because of the many common political, social and economic factors"*, p. 302, O.F. Robinson, T.D. Fergus, W.M. Gordon, *European*

a) A legal patchwork

The common law's fame and importance seem to result mainly from the English might. Indeed whereas newly formed countries have sometimes chosen the inspiring model of the *Code Civil*, most common law countries have joined this legal family because they had to, being, at some stage in their history, under British influence or rule. This common law was the result of centuries of legal sedimentation, mixes, outside influences and changes. It would be fastidious to enumerate all the traditions that influenced the common law here, but it might be interesting to mention some of them.

Legal History, 3rd Edition, Butterworths, 2000, 385 p.

What is referred to as the "common law" tradition is a little bit vague. Seen in more detail the subject seems protean. The common law of England, set up by the Norman king William the Conqueror has been a mix of rationalized English (pre-Norman) chthonic law[49] and all sorts of foreign influences.

---

[49] Following the example of H.P. Glenn, I chose to evoke "chthonic" law rather than "folk" law to avoid any ambiguities. The word chthonic comes from the Greek *kthonos* (lit.: earth) and it was used by Edward Goldsmith to describe people who live in close harmony with the earth (See *The Way : An Ecological World View*, Rider, 1992). "Chthonic" law could also be called aboriginal law. Using one word for millions of different groups does not imply that their rules were all alike, the concept of chthonic law just means that the people were living simple lives and that their laws mainly dealt with the concrete realities of these simple lives. The chthonic tradition could be said to be 2 million years old. 2 million years during which the exclusive means of subsistence of mankind were hunting and

When the Normans took over Britain, they did not try to impose new laws but rather to use and rationalize the existing chthonic law. They did the same in many other countries that they took over, including Sicily where the Norman rule accommodated itself with Islamic law[50]. In England, the Normans chose to fulfil the people's need for justice without upsetting them by repealing their traditions and rules. The king had authority over the land and guaranteed peace. The judges' main task was to see if the cases

---

gathering until the last 10.000 years during which farming and herding were developed. For H.P. Glenn *"to describe a legal tradition as chthonic is thus to attempt to describe a tradition by criteria internal to itself, as opposed to imposed criteria. (…) There was no point of origin of a chthonic legal tradition. (…) A chthonic tradition simply emerged (…) all other traditions have emerged in contrast to chthonic tradition"*. p. 57-58, *op. cit.*

[50] The Normans conquered Palermo in 1072 and ruled Sicily until the end of the following century. See p. 210, *ibid.*

brought before them corresponded to breaches of the king's peace (as defined in a list of writs[51]). Juries of locals were then used to determine (according to pre-Norman chthonic law) whether the parties' claims were founded or not. The verdict was given by the jury, in other words, by the people themselves.

This justice, rendered on a case-by-case basis, developed a rationalized set of legal principles and solutions over the centuries which were in tune with the people's lives and perpetuated in some fields the old pre-Norman traditions. Yet it was also eerily similar to the Roman manner of judging[52].

---

[51] Define the writs

[52] *"The development of the Common Law in the Middle Ages is very similar to the development of Roman Law in many points. (...) Roman Law and medieval Common Law were both dominated by 'procedural thinking'. (...) (I)n point of legal techniques the English lawyers have much more in*

As mentioned earlier, the Channel did not isolate the British Islands from the continent and goods as well as ideas circulated throughout Europe. The common law did not come into being by chance. It was a pragmatic political choice. Roman law was known and available to the Normans at the time of the conquest. Indeed William the Conqueror's own right-hand man, Lanfranc of Pavia, argued for the compatibility of Roman law and pre-conquest law[53].

Civilian influences were present in England and on the British isles at all times (Scotland for instance followed the civilian tradition). The civil law and the common law

---

common with the Roman lawyers than do the nineteenth century pandectists who expressly followed the Roman tradition" K. Zweigert, H. Kötz, p. 186, *op. cit.* - See also H.P. Glenn, p. 208, *op. cit..*

[53] See p. 213, *ibid.*

were not impervious to each other. There has indeed been a constant dialogue between the British Isles and continental Europe. There were three main vehicles of the civilian influence in England :

First of all religion, with the Catholic church's deep influence through its codified Canon Law (derived from Roman Law) and its ecclesiastical courts.

Second of all, international trade for which a mainly civilian "common" law was created[54].

Thirdly there was the academic world. Originally linked to religion, it soon became a world of its own (with a legal status for students and its own courts). The same

---

[54] The *Lex Mercatoria* (or Law Merchant) was used throughout Europe from the middle ages onwards. In England cases involving international trade were heard by the courts of admiralty, which in a common law context used methods that were mainly civilian.

courses of civil law were taught in Paris and Oxford. The use of Latin by the learned elite was another connection to the civilian tradition (conveying its legal concepts and maxims). Latin was indeed not only the language of Rome (Rome of the Empire and Rome, home of the Vatican), it was also the language of science[55].

More unexpected, yet not to be undermined are the Islamic and Jewish influences on the common law.

The Islamic influence - although long denied[56] - appears to notable. The model of the inns as law schools (which is often

---

[55] Latin was the international language that the English used to deal with their neighbours. Cf. the famous example of Irish rebel Grace O'Malley meeting queen Elizabeth I and speaking with her in Latin as none of the two spoke each other's native language.

[56] See p. 210, *ibid*.

depicted as one of the singular features of the common law[57]) was for instance imported from the Islamic world[58]. The first English inns (predecessors of the current Inns of Court)

[57] *"Whereas on the Continent legal education has always been the province of universities and consequently rather theoretical and remote from practice, in England it was the monopoly of the Inns of Court throughout the whole Middle Ages and until the nineteenth century."*, K. Zweigert, H. Kötz, p. 191, *op. cit.*

[58] *"The origin of the inn as an institution of learning in the Christian West is historically connected with London and Paris; the inns of these two cities are in turn connected historically with the Holy City of Jerusalem. This type of inn, born in Baghdad and the eastern Caliphate, had moved westward to other great cities, including Jerusalem and cities throughout Spain and Sicily"*, G. Makdisi, *The Guilds of Law in Medieval Legal History : An Inquiry into the origins of the Inns of Court*, 1985-6, Clevel. St. L. Rev. 3. – In the inns, like in the Arabic *mahadibs*, *"lawyers and aspirants lived cheek by jowl in the buildings of the guild, took their meals together, attended divine service together, made common use of the library which each Inn possessed, and joined in making music and organizing solemn feasts and dramatic entertainments"*, K. Zweigert, H. Kötz, p. 192, *op. cit.*

were modelled after the Islamic *mahadib* : law schools adjoined to mosques as living and teaching facilities[59]. Just like the *mahadib*, the inn gathered under a same roof experienced lawyers and students. The inns were the matrix in which the legal profession turned into a guild (by binding lawyers together). The inn's senior lawyers, similarly to the *mahadib*'s teachers, were quite influential in national jurisprudence[60]. With the development of the legal profession in England it was also among these lawyers that

---

[59] *"To develop the teaching necessary for the new legal professions, working in the royal courts, English lawyers eventually developed the Inns of Court (...). The earliest inns (...) were attached to churches, as the mahadib were attached to mosques"*, H.P. Glenn, *op. cit.* p. 209

[60] *"(T)he Inns of Court provided, until the middle of the seventeenth century, some doctrine which may have been almost as important as decided cases in creating the Common Law"* p. 143, O.F. Robinson, T.D. Fergus, W.M. Gordon, *op. cit.*

judges were chosen. The inns helped to structure the legal profession as a well-bound community (which did not know of the civilian distinction between academics, advocates and adjudicators).

Jewish law also influenced the common law. As explained before, the common law was originally mainly a chthonic law, a law of land. Jewish people who were excluded from farming and land-holding had turned to commerce. As a result, their Talmudic commercial law was very developed. Thus *"(w)hen English commerce began to emerge, Talmudic practices, known because of jewish-gentile commercial relations, were a natural model for common-law development"*[61].

---

[61] See H.P. Glenn p. 214, *op. cit.*

On top of these influences there was the Norman language. French was used in courts[62] until the mid-16th century. This version of French known as *"Law French"* died out by the end of the 18th century but English law retained a great quantity of its lexicon. From this perspective it would be paradoxical to argue that the principles of the common law cannot be translated into French.

b) A powerful and independent Judiciary

(1) The birth of the English Judiciary

Another very important feature of the common law is the part played by the judges. Historical circumstances seem to have favoured the establishment of a strong

---

[62] Both in the tribunals and in the monarch's entourage.

Judiciary in England. As H.P. Glenn explained, *"(t)he only avenue for a Norman legal order, common to the realm, was through a loyal judiciary. (...) There was here no loyal chthonic people, no available revelation, no corpus of learned, indigenous doctrine. So, as monarch, you could not rely on God, the people, or your own legislation"*[63]. The monarch could only rely on a corps of loyal adjudicators. *"(Y)ou couldn't name patricians, or nobles to the judicial task, as did the Romans. Your nobility could only speak French; theirs, of England, couldn't be trusted (to the extent that they had survived). So some kind of permanent judicial officer was required, who could work in a controlled and efficient manner"*[64]. The only choice left was that of priests who could read and write (and who were often trained in

---

[63] See p. 206-207, *ibid.*

[64] See p. 207, *ibid.*

canon law). They could therefore be given precise written instructions on particular cases, be asked to write down the outcome of cases they judged and thus be controlled *a priori* as well as *a posteriori*. The royal budget being - at first - modest, the number of judges was limited and they would travel around the country to settle local disputes. *"There couldn't be too many of them, or they would cost too much (...). And it would be wise to co-opt the population into their work, so if actual decisions were left to the local folks (...) then the judges could just get the right questions asked in a number of cases, and be off to another town"*[65]. Thus *"the faster, more efficient, more rational royal courts, using local knowledge, could just quietly insinuate themselves into the landscape"*[66]. The judges

---

[65] See p. 207, *ibid*.

[66] See p. 207, *ibid*.

were therefore perceived as a group distinct from the monarchy and usually not reproached with being autocratic (in contrast with their French counterparts).

(2) The judges' independence

The 1701 Act of Settlement constituted a turning point in the evolution of the English Judiciary : the judges' nominations ceased to be at the king's pleasure and became *quam diu se bene gesserint* (during good behaviour). Judges could no longer be dismissed[67] and thus gained much more power. They were picked among the experienced and prominent barristers, their careers were therefore

---

[67] Except by nearly impossible procedures: joint addresses to the two chambers of Parliament (this has never occurred in England).

already made and did not depend on how they fulfilled their adjudicating duties. They did not have to please the king and had no more reasons to be afraid of displeasing him[68]. This was a radical difference with civil law jurisdictions where judges were under the (more or less) direct control and authority of the executive[69].

---

[68] *"With judicial nomination coming closer to the end of a legal career than its beginning, there is no control of the career of a judge (as on the continent) and no effective means of dismissal. There are further elaborate guarantees of maintenance of salary, depending on the common law jurisdiction. In England there is also no present means of discipline of superior court judges, who also enjoy civil immunity in the exercise of their functions. There is no prise à partie in the common law"* See p. 225, *ibid*.

[69] In most civil law countries the careers of judge and advocate are still distinct (in France aspirant judges take the entrance exam of the *Ecole de la Magistrature* and become judges once they graduate while aspirant barristers take the bar exam). In Canada (including Québec), following the common law tradition, judges are recruited among

(3) The principle of *stare decisis*

Another element which shows the extent of the Judiciary's power in the common law tradition is the binding force of precedent, also known as the principle of *stare decisis*[70].

---

experienced barristers (10 years of experience are required).

[70] *"The doctrine lays down that every English court is bound by all decisions handed down by courts superior to it in the hierarchy; and, until quite recently, the doctrine laid down that the superior courts, namely the Court of Appeal and the House of Lords, were bound to treat their own decisions as absolutely binding. A previous decision is 'binding' in the sense that it must be followed whether it forms part of a series of similar decisions or whether it stands quite alone, whether it was handed down the previous year or a century ago, and even if the rule it lays down now seems inappropriate because of altered social circumstances or for some other reason. It had always been recognised in England that courts which were faced with the task of discovering the law should take note of previous decisions*

Often described as the main characteristic of the common law[71], this principle turns the judges into legitimate (and authoritative) creators of law. The consistency of the courts in their judgments seems like a very natural concern on the part of the people. It also seems necessary in order to establish the legitimacy of the courts (a court which would seem to be unfair could indeed not properly assert its authority and claim to render justice). *Stare decisis* therefore just seems to

---

and follow them whenever this seemed proper on the facts of the case. Indeed, given the absence of any comprehensive legislative regulation this was the only reasonable thing to do unless every individual case was to be decided denovo" See K. Zweigert, H. Kötz, p. 259-260, *op. cit.*

[71] *"According to a view expressed in England in 1934 by Goodhart, the critical difference between Continental and English methods of legal thinking lies in the doctrine of the binding force of precedent (...). At first sight this view seems plausible even today."* See K. Zweigert, H. Kötz, p. 259, *op. cit.*

result from common sense. Yet this principle has advantages as well as disadvantages. Depending on one's views, the judges' ability to create legal principles could be considered to be either of the two. Moreover, the binding force of precedent might compel a judge to apply a precedent which has become unsatisfactory (e.g. because of changes in the context) or which s/he finds unfair (the principle of *stare decisis* implies fairness in judgments - the vast majority of the courts do not have the power to overrule a judgment coming from a court at the top of the hierarchy and even the highest court is not supposed to overrule its own decisions[72]). There are ways to go around the principle of *stare decisis*[73] but can they always be resorted to ?

---

[72] Cf. footnote 82

[73] Common Law judges can nonetheless avoid unsatisfactory

As explained above[74] the post-revolutionary civil law tradition was firmly opposed to that kind of leeway on the part of the judges. The binding force of the precedent could therefore be said to be more of a common law concept (it should nonetheless be noted that it is not absent in the civilian tradition[75]).

---

precedents by distinguishing the present case from the precedent. A previous decision is binding only where the basic reason underlying the decision (the *ratio decidendi*) covers the instant dispute.

[74] See Chapter 1, paragraph 1.3

[75] For instance when appellate jurisdictions make it clear that they interpret this or that law in a certain way and will overturn decisions based on a diverging interpretation, they send out a clear incentive to lower courts to follow their interpretation. Lower courts do not have to follow it, but it could seem pointless not to.

c) A pragmatic and concrete law

(1) The communal character of the common law

The common law was – in the first place – a casuistic way of settling disputes.

As explained above[76], it was not originally a law of "rights" focused on the individual but rather a law of the community, centred on relations and mutual obligations[77]. The English Judiciary was never strongly contested or perceived as a despotic body[78]

---

[76] See Chapter 1, paragraph 1.2

[77] Cf. *"A law of relations, of mutual obligations, is not a law which concentrates its attention on the legal powers or interests of the individual. It is not a law of rights, and the notion of subjective right (as they say in civilian language) played little or no role in the history of the common law in England."* p.220 in H. Patrick Glenn, *Legal Traditions of the World*, O.U.P., 2000, 371 p.

[78] *"(the English judges) were never the object of physical*

while on the continent *"rights were developed as an important instrument in overcoming feudal hierarchy"* [79]. In England, *"(r)ights were not necessary in doing this, and in the beginning would even have presented a jarring, discordant note in the process of faithfully reflecting the society"*[80]. Even though there were big inequalities in England, *"the society had lots of instruments other than law to bring about change in itself. And the common law could itself be altered in ways contributing to equality, liberty and right, without renouncing its explicitly communal character"*[81].

---

attack (except for the odd brickbat, which the contempt power expeditiously dealt with). They were never seen as part of a hostile and distant autocracy in the way, say, the French judiciary was" p.220 in H. Patrick Glenn, *Legal Traditions of the World*, O.U.P., 2000, 371 p.

[79] See H.P. Glenn, p. 220, *op. cit.*
[80] See H.P. Glenn, p. 220, *op. cit.*
[81] See H.P. Glenn, p. 220, *op. cit.*

(2) The forms of action: the writs

Devoid of this notion of rights, medieval common law seems to have been dominated by procedural thinking[82]. The context led legal practitioners to think not so much in terms of rights as in terms of types of actions. They were more interested in the concrete facts which fell within the various actions or writs rather than in elaborating the substantive law into a rational system[83]. They

---

[82] *"(the method of common lawyers) is intensely casuistic. They proceed from case to case, being more anxious to establish a good working set of rules, even at the risk of some logical incoherence which may, sooner or later, create a difficulty, than to set up anything like a logical system."* Buckland & McNair, Roman Law and Common Law, cited by K. Zweigert, H. Kötz p. 186-187, *op. cit.*

[83] See K. Zweigert, H. Kötz, p. 186, *op. cit.*

are one of the key elements of the common law.

The requirement of a writ was only abolished in 1832. The forms of action were a mould that shaped the common law and their influence can still be felt in today[84].

---

[84] *"In Maitland's wonderful language, "The forms of action we have buried, but they still rule us from their graves." This wasn't just sleight of hand. If you think of the writs and forms of action as a kind of visible mould, shaping though concealing the secreted law, removal of the mould leaves the revealed substance beneath. Where you could previously get to the jury, and win if they believed you, it can now be said that you are entitled as a matter of substantive law (or more probably, that the defendant is obliged towards you as a matter of substantive law). So though the procedural reforms are fundamental in the history of the common law, they also provided a bridge between the old processual world and the new substantive world. The new substantive law bears all the marks, and uses much of the language, of the old writs."* See p. 224, H. Patrick Glenn, *Legal Traditions of the World*, O.U.P., 2000

3. The Canadian mix

It should be noted that while Québec (and on some level Canada) can be considered a mixed jurisdiction, it is a mix of the French pre-revolutionary legal tradition and the English common law. It should be remembered that Canada only became fully independent from England in 1982[85]. The ties with England are still strong and Queen Elizabeth II of Britain is still the (official) head of state of Canada.

The Canadian mix was subsequently enriched continuously by the influence of the U.S.A. and that of French thought.

(1) New France's legacy in Québec

---

[85] Through the 1982 *Constitution Act*.

aa) French customary law

The use of French law in Canada dates back to Jacques Cartier's discovery of the Saint Lawrence River in 1534. Being a Breton, he applied the customs of Brittany to settle disputes[86]. Likewise, the subsequent settlers applied the customs of their areas of origin. It is therefore not one French judicial model which was exported to Canada but several. Indeed until the 16th century French law was composed of different customary law systems bound together by political and ecclesiastical ties. In the 16th century French law moved from being a community-based law to being a national law applying directly to equal and autonomous citizens[87].

---

[86] See M.F. Joüou des Longrais, *Jacques Cartier juriste – La très ancienne coutume de Bretagne de Jacques Cartier*, in *Le droit civil français*, p. 943-946

[87] Equality is meant

Community-based law was predominant in French Canada during the 16th and 17th centuries[88]. At that time *"French customs were received, in all their diversity in an informal way, depending on the origins of the settlers"*[89]. The local institutions were not very developed or autonomous, *"a lot of energy (was) put in general management, in fur trade, in agriculture, in aboriginal relations – very little (was) done in the field of justice"*[90]. The seigniorial system was set up in New France. A social system in which the individual's position was defined by customs.

---

[88] See p. 579, H.P. Glenn, *Droit Québécois et Droit Français: Communauté, Autonomie, Concordance*, Ed° Yvon Blais Inc. (Cowansville, Québec), 1993, 597 p.

[89] See p. 579, H.P. Glenn, *Droit Québécois et Droit Français: Communauté, Autonomie, Concordance*, Ed° Yvon Blais Inc. (Cowansville, Québec), 1993, 597 p.

[90] See p. 579-580, H.P. Glenn, *Droit Québécois et Droit Français: Communauté, Autonomie, Concordance*, Ed° Yvon Blais Inc. (Cowansville, Québec), 1993, 597 p.

French customary law existed alongside aboriginal customs which were tolerated[91].

In 1664, Minister Colbert created the Company of the West Indies. The Company was granted a monopoly on fur trade. Pursuant to the Charter of the Company, the custom of Paris became the official custom of New France, superseding all others.

This constitutes the bulk of the French legal legacy. Although in the 17th century, the custom of Paris had already been modified in order to better suit the Canadian context, it was never fully erased or given up, only partially altered through the years.

---

[91] *"French customary law, in its 'primitive purity' (…) coexists with aboriginal customs. Several decisions of the Superior Council deal with their respective roles"* p. 580, H.P. Glenn, *Droit Québécois et Droit Français: Communauté, Autonomie, Concordance*, Ed° Yvon Blais Inc. (Cowansville, Québec), 1993, 597 p.

While French law shifted from a community-based tradition to an autonomous tradition, the law of French-speaking Canada remained community-based.

The seigniorial system, which had been annihilated by the revolution in France, remained in place in French-speaking Canada until the middle of the 19th century.

The law of Québec has retained many concepts of old French law which disappeared long time ago in France[92]. Religious marriages are still recognized in Québec while in France only non-religious marriages are recognised by the state since the French revolution. Exceptions coming from the formulary procedure of Roman Law which were

---

[92] For instance the emphytéose, the substitutions fidécommissaires... See p. 580, H.P. Glenn, *Droit Québécois et Droit Français: Communauté, Autonomie, Concordance*, Ed° Yvon Blais Inc. (Cowansville, Québec), 1993, 597 p.

abandoned in France are featured in Québec's current Civil Procedure Code.

bb) The roots of bilingualism in Québec: "Speak French and we shall obey"

As will be detailed later, when the Canadian territories of New France became English, they were still under the rule of absolute monarchy. There were no real counter-powers in place in French Canada. No freedom of expression either.

While many French-Canadian loyalists fought hard to defeat the English, Westminter's rule did not bring with it the threat of terror and autocracy. The British model was indeed at that time seen by many French thinkers (such as Montesquieu[93]) as a

---

[93] In *De l'Esprit des Lois* (*The Spirit of Laws*), the baron of

progressive one. The British Parliament inspired the early French revolutionaries. So nationalism (and Anglo-French rivalry) left aside, the new Canadian government was not as authoritarian as the former French one[94]. But a striking difference was that the local French-Canadian notables lost their prominence. In the early years of the English

---

Montesquieu pleaded for the separation of powers and described the British institutions in detail. They were, in his eyes a good and successful example of a system where powers limit each other, where checks and balances prevent the institutions from falling into the excesses of despotism.

[94] *"The true glory of a conquering King is to provide the defeated with the same happiness and tranquillity in their Religion as well as in the possession of their properties as they enjoyed before being defeated: We have enjoyed this tranquillity during the War itself, it has increased since Peace has been brought."* – Petition of French Canadian notables to the English King made in 1763 (four years after French Canada became English), in Guy Bourthillier, Jean Meynaud, p. 97, *Le Choc des langues au Québec*, Les Presses de l'Université du Québec, 1972, 768 p.

rule, they were lost in translation. The Québécois merchants and the French-Canadian legal profession were shaken by this systemic change, which relegated them to subaltern positions. They were soon challenged and replaced by English-Canadian merchants.

In 1763, four years after the beginning of the English rule in Canada, French-Canadian notables petitioned the King demanding that English law be translated into French and justice rendered in French[95].

---

[95] *"For four years now we have enjoyed the greatest tranquillity. What upheaval is now depriving us of it? on the part of four or five Lawyers, whose character we respect, but who do not understand our language, and who expect that as soon as they have spoken we should comprehend Constitutions that they have not yet explained to us and by which we will always be willing to abide when we shall know their content; but how should we get to know them if they are not translated in our language?"*, See Guy Bourthillier, Jean Meynaud, p. 97, *Le Choc des langues au Québec*, Les

What the French-Canadians obtained from this petition was the right to use their language in official proceedings and to have the laws translated into French. The French-Canadians basically told the King: *"speak French and we shall obey"*[96]. Besides the combination of the civil law and the common law a key ingredient of the Canadian mix was therefore language.

It is important to note that this linguistic element has been there as soon as the British took over the Canadian territories of New France.

As will be explained later, this bilingualism was not always effective or efficient. But it was a distinctive feature of

Presses de l'Université du Québec, 1972, 768 p.

[96] See Guy Bourthillier, Jean Meynaud, p. 97, *Le Choc des langues au Québec*, Les Presses de l'Université du Québec, 1972, 768 p.

(Quebec and) Canadian law. While most of the law in English-speaking Canada and on the federal scale is of an Anglo-saxon inspiration consistent with the common law tradition, the use of the French language (and the history behind it) has made its law unique.

cc) The mix of old French law and English law

Through the 18th and 19th centuries, many jurists of French-speaking Canada fought to protect the old French law. *"The struggle was of course directed against the influence of the common law, but also against the influence of the new egalitarian and modern French law"*[97]. These jurists sought to

---

[97] See p. 581, H.P. Glenn, *Droit Québécois et Droit Français: Communauté, Autonomie, Concordance*, Ed° Yvon Blais Inc.

maintain the old law (*"the influence of the Church is evident through all this period"*[98]) but also – through these traditions – to express an attachment to their community. As will be explained later, the law, just like the language is one of the elements that Québec built its identity on.

English law was brought to Québec with the British rule from 1759 onwards. The new rulers sought to set up a familiar judicial order whose members would be loyal to the crown. The French Canadians resisted. This resulted in a situation where some of the English law was incorporated and some of the French law was allowed to remain in place.

(Cowansville, Québec), 1993, 597 p.

[98] See p. 581, H.P. Glenn, *Droit Québécois et Droit Français: Communauté, Autonomie, Concordance*, Ed° Yvon Blais Inc. (Cowansville, Québec), 1993, 597 p.

The English law was incorporated in the fields related to government and police, i.e. public law (especially constitutional law), administrative law and penal law. Private law (more precisely matters of *"property and civil rights"*[99]) remained mainly French. In some fields of private law, English principles were also included, such as the rules of evidence in commercial matters, or trials by juries.

In the 18th century French law was still deeply rooted in customs but renewed/rediscovered Roman law was becoming more present in the field of obligations and codifying ordinances existed in the fields of procedure, trade, donations, testaments and marine. *"The customary tradition was losing its prominence in a larger*

---

[99] Mainly old French law as provided by the 1774 *Québec Act*.

process of creation of a national law in France"[100].

"*Although the law remained customary in many fields, it was a substantial law, addressed directly to individuals, and could thus be redacted formally in the 16th century. (...) (T)his customary law (was) modern in its structuring elements. It (was) open to rationalisation – this (was) made manifest by its written form from the 16th century onwards and the control of its application by courts of appeal*"[101].

In contrast, the common law tradition was still defined by the mould established by the Normans between the 11th and 13th

---

[100] See p. 581, H.P. Glenn, *Droit Québécois et Droit Français: Communauté, Autonomie, Concordance*, Ed° Yvon Blais Inc. (Cowansville, Québec), 1993, 597 p.

[101] See p. 589, H.P. Glenn, *Droit Québécois et Droit Français: Communauté, Autonomie, Concordance*, Ed° Yvon Blais Inc. (Cowansville, Québec), 1993, 597 p.

centuries: the access to courts was restricted[102], defined by forms of action, the juries based their decisions on non-written criteria. *"The French law established in New France (was), because of its structure, an essentially modern law; the English law (was) essentially medieval"*[103].

The English law imposed itself in fields where no resistance could exist (the state, the government) but it had a hard time imposing itself in other fields[104]. English penal law was

---

[102] In France the general access to courts is granted to citizens since the 13th century. – See See p. 588, H.P. Glenn, *Droit Québécois et Droit Français: Communauté, Autonomie, Concordance*, Ed° Yvon Blais Inc. (Cowansville, Québec), 1993, 597 p.

[103] p. 589, H.P. Glenn, *Droit Québécois et Droit Français: Communauté, Autonomie, Concordance*, Ed° Yvon Blais Inc. (Cowansville, Québec), 1993, 597 p.

[104] For instance, the requirement of a brief of authorisation to start an action was introduced in 1777 but abolished for

not welcomed and French Canadians resisted its incorporation with a lot of energy.

English private law had nonetheless an influence in several fields. French Canadian traders soon adapted to the practices of English commercial law, which governed all the trade on the continent. In 1774 traders got the English commercial law of evidence and trials by juries to be formally incorporated into French Canadian law.

The English procedure progressively became the norm. For a long time (under the British rule), the people designated to be

---

being a cumbersome formality in 1801. Another example is that of appeal which was restricted to the sole executive council in 1763 and restored to its previous form (before courts of appeal) in 1793. – See p. 590, H.P. Glenn, *Droit Québécois et Droit Français: Communauté, Autonomie, Concordance*, Ed° Yvon Blais Inc. (Cowansville, Québec), 1993

judges were English-speakers trained in (common) law and unfamiliar with the continental procedure. The role of the judge was more reduced than in the French tradition, he was just in charge of controlling the access to the jury, which would then establish the truth and make the final decision.

The creation of the bar resulted from this change as advocates were now required by the adversarial procedure. *"Naturally, once it was established, the bar protected its role in the administration of justice"*[105].

Thus the formerly civilian jurisdiction of New France saw the progressive introduction of procedural methods conceived for a system of forms of action devoid of substantial law

---

[105] See p. 584, H.P. Glenn, *Droit Québécois et Droit Français: Communauté, Autonomie, Concordance*, Ed° Yvon Blais Inc. (Cowansville, Québec), 1993, 597 p.

with judges whose powers were limited. While a large share of New France's (now Québec's) law remained French, while a large number of legal concepts survived, the common law replaced or transformed it in many fields, making it a *sui generis* mixed jurisdiction.

(2) The continuity of French and English influences in Québec

Since the beginning of the British rule, Québec has been a mixed jurisdiction. The civilian elements were not limited to the legacy of New France as Québec was continuously enriched by modern French law and jurisprudence. The same could be said of

English law whose influence remains considerable in Québec.

aa) The extra-territorial sources of law

The French approach which considers the state (through the legislator) to be the only true (and legitimate) source of law has not been received in Québec. While in France, this approach was developed mainly after the revolution, in Québec *"the local sources of the law (...) were and remain today too multiform to allow the reception of the modern French conception of law"*[106].

In New France the customs (first the various local customs, later the customs of

---

[106] See p. 585, H.P. Glenn, *Droit Québécois et Droit Français: Communauté, Autonomie, Concordance*, Ed° Yvon Blais Inc. (Cowansville, Québec), 1993, 597 p.

Paris) existed alongside the case-law of the *Conseil Supérieur* and the local legislation. The sources of the law were multiple.

"*The English regime reinforced the notion of multiplicity of local sources in the law of Québec*"[107]. With the British came the British legislative style (longer statutes, more complex phrasing), which did not give the legislator a bigger influence. Case-law was given more importance in theory, but not in practice (as the 19th century judges were accused of corruption[108]). The principle of *stare decisis* was not received in Québec

---

[107] See p. 585, H.P. Glenn, *Droit Québécois et Droit Français: Communauté, Autonomie, Concordance*, Ed° Yvon Blais Inc. (Cowansville, Québec), 1993, 597 p.

[108] The accusations were such that, "*in an effort to define the role of the judiciary, the judges were deprived of the right to vote*". – See p. 585, H.P. Glenn, *Droit Québécois et Droit Français: Communauté, Autonomie, Concordance*, Ed° Yvon Blais Inc. (Cowansville, Québec), 1993, 597 p.

where the 1866 codification prevented its reception.

The role played by legislation and codes became more important in the following years. The 1866 *Civil Code of Lower Canada* and the 1867 *Code of civil procedure* (or the following codes[109]) did not abolish pre-existing French law. They even incorporated some elements of the contemporary French law[110].

---

[109] The 1994 Civil Code of Québec, the 1897 and 1966 codes of civil procedure did not abolish pre-existing French law (such as the *Code Louis* for example).

[110] *"Even before the codification of the civil law in 1866, Québec's law was following the modern trends of civil law. A big share of the French law of obligations was received in New France through the writings of Pothier. The 1866 Civil Code could thus follow a big part of the Code Napoléon – which was also shaped by this pre-revolutionary modernisation"* – See p. 590, H.P. Glenn, *Droit Québécois et Droit Français: Communauté, Autonomie, Concordance*, Ed° Yvon Blais Inc. (Cowansville, Québec), 1993, 597 p.

The local sources of the law in Québec are multiple and extra-territorial sources such as the French ones have been (and are) continuously resorted to.

These resorts although frequent are not subject to particular rules. *"In the 19th century, it is French jurisprudence on the Code Napoléon, which became in Québec an important source concerning the content... of ancient French law. (...) It is not due to the merits of its style or content, it is because it represents what is Québec law, at least within its non-revolutionary parts"*[111]. The British authorities did not stand in the way of this practice, on the contrary the Judicial Committee of the Privy Council perfectly

---

[111] See p. 586, H.P. Glenn, *Droit Québécois et Droit Français: Communauté, Autonomie, Concordance*, Ed° Yvon Blais Inc. (Cowansville, Québec), 1993, 597 p.

accepted that ancient law could thus be revivified[112].

Apart from the courts, it is also Québec's budding jurisprudence which got a large share of its inspiration from French jurisprudence. Among all the French sources of law, only contemporary case-law was rarely resorted to (first of all because it dealt more with new French law than ancient French law and secondly because – for a long time – it represented big quantities of books whose exportation was quite costly[113]). By resorting to extra-territorial sources, *"one implicitly indicates that local sources are incomplete"*[114].

---

[112] See p. 586, H.P. Glenn, *Droit Québécois et Droit Français: Communauté, Autonomie, Concordance*, Ed° Yvon Blais Inc. (Cowansville, Québec), 1993, 597 p.

[113] See p. 586, H.P. Glenn, *Droit Québécois et Droit Français: Communauté, Autonomie, Concordance*, Ed° Yvon Blais Inc. (Cowansville, Québec), 1993, 597 p.

[114] See p. 586, H.P. Glenn, *Droit Québécois et Droit Français: Communauté, Autonomie, Concordance*, Ed° Yvon Blais Inc.

These resorts could be justified by the fact that the French Canadians felt that they were still – on some level – part of the French community (although they did not share the experience and ideals of the French revolution). It could also be justified by the refusal to admit the plenitude of local sources; in that case one could find a connection to the British approach here: common lawyers seek the meaning of the law beyond the words and look into the genesis of legal principles in order to understand them – while civilians usually tend to stick more to the law as it is phrased. It is hard to know which of these two explanations is the most appropriate. They are not exclusive of each other (or of other explanations).

Resorts to French sources were continuous during the 19th and 20th centuries

---

(Cowansville, Québec), 1993, 597 p.

and it are likely to continue during the 21st century as well. Yet *"the role of French jurisprudence in contemporary Québec law seems more precarious than before"*[115]. The number of citations of French jurisprudence in court decisions can be a good indicator of the French influence.

The figures speak for themselves. Between 1900 and 1939, French jurisprudence was cited in 42% of court decisions made in Québec. Between 1940 and 1969 this rate was dropped to 29% and it finally to 16% between 1970 and 1990[116].

---

[115] p. 595, H.P. Glenn, *Droit Québécois et Droit Français: Communauté, Autonomie, Concordance*, Ed° Yvon Blais Inc. (Cowansville, Québec), 1993, 597 p.

[116] p. 595, H.P. Glenn, *Droit Québécois et Droit Français: Communauté, Autonomie, Concordance*, Ed° Yvon Blais Inc. (Cowansville, Québec), 1993, 597 p.

It is important to note that French sources were not the only extra-territorial sources that jurists resorted to. *"For the texts of the 1866 Civil Code of Lower Canada whose origin is to be found in English law, the rule of interpretation which (was) developed (precised) that English law (was) the best guide"*[117].

bb) Continuity and identity in Québec's new Civil Code

The first civil code made in French Canada was the aforementioned Civil *Code of Lower Canada*. It soon became one of the symbols of the French Canadian identity: *"an*

---

[117] See p. 586-7, H.P. Glenn, *Droit Québécois et Droit Français: Communauté, Autonomie, Concordance*, Ed° Yvon Blais Inc. (Cowansville, Québec), 1993, 597 p.

identity (which was) autonomous from the common law and even from the French law"[118].

A new Code came into force in 1994. This Code resembles its predecessors and French codes in many ways. *"The same family likeness is present. Nevertheless, the text of the new Civil Code being the second codification of the civil law done in Québec, and the codifier having been influenced by several foreign models, the new Code presents a specific identity, a more marked autonomy than the Civil Code of Lower Canada"*[119].

The 1994 *Civil Code of Québec* has a big number of foreign sources. Out of 990 major

---

[118] p. 593, H.P. Glenn, *Droit Québécois et Droit Français: Communauté, Autonomie, Concordance*, Ed° Yvon Blais Inc. (Cowansville, Québec), 1993, 597 p.

[119] p. 594, H.P. Glenn, *Droit Québécois et Droit Français: Communauté, Autonomie, Concordance*, Ed° Yvon Blais Inc. (Cowansville, Québec), 1993, 597 p.

foreign sources[120] of the new Code, 465 come from the common law (mainly in the field of obligations – especially in maritime law) and 338 come from French law[121]. One should note that references to French law were only made in situations where resort to French law would not be implied by the current law, these 338 references are therefore mainly innovations borrowed from contemporary French law. *"The essence of the Code remains deeply French in its inspiration; tracing the French origins of most of the articles would have been fastidious"*[122].

---

[120] Foreign sources of national law cited as pertinent sources of the new Civil Code by the ministry of Justice in its commentary.

[121] See p. 587, H.P. Glenn, *Droit Québécois et Droit Français: Communauté, Autonomie, Concordance*, Ed° Yvon Blais Inc. (Cowansville, Québec), 1993, 597 p.

[122] See p. 587, H.P. Glenn, *Droit Québécois et Droit Français: Communauté, Autonomie, Concordance*, Ed° Yvon Blais Inc. (Cowansville, Québec), 1993, 597 p.

The promulgation of the Civil Code of Quebec in 1994 was arguably one of the most important events in the history of Quebec and Canadian civil law[123]. The previous civil code had been in force for more than 125 years and this new version was firstly intended to update it. This new code illustrates the adaptation of civil law to contemporary Quebec. It has also *"confirmed the identity-creating function of the civil law tradition, which was introduced into New France more than three centuries previously"*[124].

---

[123] See Roderick Macdonald, *"Encoding Canadian Civil Law"* in *"The Harmonization of Federal Legislation with Quebec Civil Law and Canadian Bijuralism: Collection of Studies"* (Ottawa: Department of Justice Canada, 1997), p.170.

[124] See p. 5, Mélanie Brunet, *Out of the Shadows: The Civil Law Tradition in the Department of Justice Canada*, Department of Justice Canada (Ottawa, 2000)

French and English law have had and continue to have a big influence on the law of Québec. *"It would not be realistic to see in the contrast between these two traditions the necessity of making a final choice for one or the other, or the possibility of one triumphing over the other. They are rather components of a larger process, that of legal practice. (...) The interaction between these two traditions (...) reflects (...) their presence and their vigour at the decision-making level in the practice of law. The jurist is constantly faced with such choices. As a jurist, he avoids to make a definitive choice. A family too allows a lot of diversity"*[125].

---

[125] See p. 596-597, H.P. Glenn, *Droit Québécois et Droit Français: Communauté, Autonomie, Concordance*, Ed° Yvon Blais Inc. (Cowansville, Québec), 1993

(3) The United States' influence

Although Canada is an immense country, its whole population is equivalent to that of California. Canada's powerful and very populated neighbour has a tremendous influence on the country's culture as well as economy. As Canadian Prime Minister Pierre Eliott Trudeau declared before the U.S. Congress: *"Living next to you is in some ways like sleeping with an elephant: No matter how friendly and even-tempered the beast, one is affected by every twitch and grunt"*[126].

The difference in size has resulted in a disproportion in terms of influence: the U.S.A. influence Canada much more than Canada influences the U.S.A. This influence is to be felt in all fields, including law.

---

[126] Cited by Priit J. Vesilund in *Common Ground, Different Dreams*, National Geographic, February 2000.

It is not uncommon for justices of the Canadian Supreme Court to cite their American counterparts[127]. It is not uncommon for Canadian legal academics to do all or part of their legal studies in the U.S.A.[128]. Nor is it uncommon for jurists and judges to refer to the American Supreme Court[129].

[127] Occurrences are be too numerous to mention. When reading Canadian jurisprudence especially articles written by Canadian judges, one notices how famous the landmark cases of the Supreme Court of the United States are.

[128] This seems to have an immediate influence on the Canadian approach to law. *"Lately, (...) as Canadians have come to take their LL.M.'s in the US rather than in the UK, one notices an increasing tendency for legal academics to trumpet the forty-year-old insights of American legal realism with all the fervor of an immediate revelation from heaven"*, in Bell, D.G., *The birth of Canadian legal history*,

[129] In a speech at the Canada – United States Law Institute, Canadian academic Peter H. Russell explained that *"as a close neighbour my main complaint about your Supreme Court is that so dazzling is its light that we in Canada are too often blinded to the significant and distinctive features of our own Supreme Court"*, See p. 4, Peter H. Russell,

One of the notable American influences could be the popularisation of the concept of fundamental rights as well as its corollary: the idea that these rights have to be enshrined in a text of supra-statutory value. The *Canadian Charter of Rights and Freedoms* is seen by many as the result of the American influence on Canada[130]. At the time it was passed no

---

Introduction: History and Development of the Court in National Society - The Canadian Supreme Court, 3 Can. – U.S. L.J. 4, 1980

[130] "*During the second half of the 20th century Québec and Canada have endowed themselves with Charters of individual rights and freedoms whose application is attributed to general courts. The American influence is evident here*". See p. 592, H.P. Glenn, *Droit Québécois et Droit Français: Communauté, Autonomie, Concordance*, Ed° Yvon Blais Inc. (Cowansville, Québec), 1993, 597 p. – Some could argue that these Charters echo the 1789 *Declaration of the Rights of Man and of the Citizen* made during the French revolution. One should bear in mind the fact that this very Declaration was inspired by American sources (such as

equivalent piece of legislation existed in England[131].

American law also exerts a great influence in the field of trade. As explained above, Anglo-American commercial law governs trade in Canada (including Québec[132]) . For many years, the United States and Canada have enjoyed a privileged commercial partnership. In 1989 their agreed to eliminate

---

the 1776 *Constitution of Virginia*).

[131] The first similar piece of legislation incorporated in English law was the Human Rights Act

[132] In commercial matters, since the British took over the Canadian territories of New France, they took the lead in commerce (and the English commercial law imposed itself). In French Canada, the French Code de Commerce did not have the success in terms of prestige or influence as the Code Napoléon, *"in commercial law (...) the reference is nowadays Anglo-American law"*. – See p. 592, H.P. Glenn, *Droit Québécois et Droit Français: Communauté, Autonomie, Concordance*, Ed° Yvon Blais Inc. (Cowansville, Québec), 1993, 597 p.

or reduce their tariffs. This agreement was the basis of the 1992 North American Free Trade Agreement (N.A.F.T.A.), which created a free-trade zone between Canada, the U.S.A. and Mexico. For Canada, being a party to the N.A.F.T.A. had legal consequences in various fields (commercial law, labour law, intellectual property law, environment law)[133].

(4) The lost Aboriginal legacy

Canada's native peoples have never been given a leading role in legislation or justice under the French and British rules. As Canada became a country of its own (with the 1867 *British North America Act*, through which

---

[133] The influence of the N.A.F.T.A. has been presented in the subpart on the influence of the United States because although three countries are party to this agreement, the major actor here is the United States.

it acquired the status British dominion[134]) Aboriginals progressively gained recognition.

The early settlers had signed treaties with the Aboriginals allowing them to live according to their traditions and laws (which varied from nation to nation). These rights were more or less protected over the centuries (at times more, at times less) insofar as they did not contravene with the laws or interests of the federal and provincial governments.

The Canadian approach to the Aboriginal question seems to have been one-sided. Rebuilding trust, restoring respect, healing the wounds of the past were the main motivations behind this approach. Aboriginal traditions are now protected but they have

---

[134] Dominions were self-governing territories within the British empire.

very little influence on the rest of Canadian law.

The creation in 1999 of the province of Nunavut following an application by the Inuit people might allow this nation to develop a different approach to law and influence the rest of Canada. There are also good chances that the influence goes the other way round and that Nunavut's approach to legislation replicates that of the other provinces. The Canadian constitution guarantees a certain number of rights to all Canadian citizens and thus also puts limits to the provincial legislative activities. Although it has the status of province, Nunavut is still a new and has a very small population.

It seems that what could have been an Aboriginal influence in law has been lost long time ago as the Aboriginals were excluded from Canadian society.

(5) Towards a bijural legal education in Canada

Legal education of civil lawyers and common lawyers is arguably quite distinct in terms of approach, techniques and knowledge[135]

---

[135] Xavier Blanc-Jouvan, head of the bijural curriculum at the Université Paris 1 – Sorbonne, laments the narrow-mindedness of monojural education. *"I dream of a book that would introduce students to the law in general, and not only to the civil law, as is the case at present. The books we now have in France under titles such as "Introduction to the Law" immediately convey the idea that law is a system of rules imposed by the state, mostly through legislation. They do not even mention case law as a source of law; rather they relegate decisions of the courts to the lesser status of an authority. This puts the student in an awkward position when he tries to understand the spirit of the common law. Similar books published in England start identifying the law with the common law, and they give a long description of the formation of this common law and*

. For legal comparatist Nicholas Kasirer, *"both civilians and common lawyers have very often treated their own backyards as the universe in thinking that all law is their law"*[136]. In recent years, several Canadian universities[137] have made efforts to bridge this cultural gap by setting up bijural curricula[138]. These curricula

later of equity, minimizing the role of legislation until one comes to the nineteenth century. Is it really so hard to speak the same language to all first-year law students ?", See p. 63-64, Xavier Blanc-Jouvan, *Bijuralism in legal education - A French view*, 52 J. Legal Educ. 61-67, 2002.

[136] See p. 40, Nicholas Kasirer, *Bijuralism in Law's Empire and Law's Cosmos*, 52 J. Legal Educ. 29-41, 2002

[137] The majority of Canadian universities do not offer bijural curricula (yet) but the major universities do. The university of McGill in Montreal and the university of Ottawa were the first to launch such curricula.

[138] Lawyers trained in both the civil law and the common law will arguably have a different approach to both traditions. For Nicholas Kasirer a bijural education allows students to become familiar with each tradition's mindset. *"(T)he civilian character of the legal idea appears most plainly when it is discovered through a knowledge-based*

allowed students to receive a dual training in both civil law and common law.

This trend will produce new generations of bilingual lawyers familiar with both of Canada's legal traditions. These new generations who will be familiar with the mindset of both traditions, might bring the commonalities of civil law and common law to the fore. This will – in the long run – favour the convergence of these traditions[139].

---

encounter with the common law. Where the comparison turns on the informational plane of rules and outcomes, bijuralism is reduced to the intellectual equivalent of comparing the Paris and London phone books. But where the comparative endeavor proceeds cosmologically so that the civil law is presented as one mentalité or epistemology for law, in conversation with another mindset, bijuralism takes up its natural place as an ideas-based study wherein the civil law is treated as an intellectual tradition rather than a compendium of rules contained or not in a code". – See p. 39, Nicholas Kasirer, *Bijuralism in Law's Empire and Law's Cosmos*, 52 J. Legal Educ. 29-41, 2002

[139] The teaching of both the common law and civil

law might even, according to Louis Perret, Dean of the Law School at the University of Ottawa, contribute to the creation of a new international *jus commune*. – See p. 734-736, Louis Perret, *De la nécessité d'enseigner le droit civil et la common law dans les Facultés de droit au Canada*, 31 Revue Générale de Droit, 731-740, 2001.

IV. LANGUAGE LAWS IN CANADA: FROM TOLERANCE TO RECOGNITION

Nowadays, while Canada has two official languages, only 18% of Canadians are actually bilingual[140]. Moreover English and French are recognized as the official languages of the federal Canadian state but only the province New Brunswick[141] is officially and in practice bilingual while the other nine provinces and the three territories are not.

---

[140] It is also quite interesting to note that there are more bilingual people among French-speakers than among English-speakers. According to the 1996 census 41% of native French-speakers are able to converse in both official languages while only 9% of native English-speakers are.

[141] New Brunswick is the only province apart from Québec which has a large proportion of French-speaker. In the 2001 Canadian population census, 32,9% of the inhabitants of the province declared French as their mother tongue. New Brunswick's official bilingualism is enshrined in section 16 of the Canadian Charter of Rights and Freedoms.

Official bilingualism is therefore limited to matters related to the federal state and fundamental rights.

1. *A first step towards official bilingualism: the British North America Act (1867)*

Official bilingualism dates back to the 1867 *British North America Act* (also known as the 1867 *Constitution Act*) which established a new country called Canada with four provinces: Ontario, Québec, New Brunswick and Nova Scotia.

Its section 133 allowed the use of both French and English for parliamentary debates and proceedings before federal courts. Both languages had to be used in the records and journals of the federal parliament. Its laws had to be enacted and published in both languages. The *B.N.A. Act* is not a mere Act of Parliament, it is the first component of the Canadian Constitution. Bilingualism has therefore been a constitutional principle in Canada since the *B.N.A. Act*.

Section 133 also established both English and French as the official languages of the Quebec legislature and Courts; the same conditions applied to Manitoba when it entered Confederation in 1870. These two provinces had indeed a significant proportion of Francophones.

No obligation of bilingualism was imposed on the other provinces. The *B.N.A. Act* turned French into an official language of the federal state but weighed on the Francophones by not granting Québec the right to be an unilingual province too.

Despite French having official language status, its use was curtailed in many fields. English became the day-to-day language of the federal Parliament and courts. Very few English-speaking MPs or lawyers spoke French so the Francophone minority usually resorted to English. During the first century of the existence of Canada (as established by the *B.N.A. Act*), only 2% of the Parliamentary debates took place in French[142]. The Government published federal statutes and parliamentary records in both languages but the French version was usually a mere translation whose publication was delayed. Many other government documents and subordinate legislation not mentioned in

---

[142] See Edmund A. Aungier, *Language Legislation and Official Bilingualism: the uneasy coexistence of Canada's language communities* in *Canada, Confederation to Present, An interactive history of Canada*, CD-Rom, Chinook Publications (Edmonton, Alberta), 2001

section 133 of the *B.N.A. Act* were published in English only.

It is only in the 20th century that postage stamps (1927) and bank notes[143] (1936) became bilingual. French was not spoken at the Supreme Court until 1944 with the appointment of Thibaudeau Rinfret as Chief Justice (and even then French was rarely used). Many English-speaking provinces decided not to provide education in French[144].

In the field of federal politics steps were taken very slowly. The federal translation bureau was only established in 1934 and simultaneous interpretation of the debates at the House of Commons only began in 1954.

---

[143] Bank notes became bilingual after an experiment of printing two separate currencies which proved too expensive. -

[144] Cf. The Manitoba Schools Question and Regulation 17 in Ontario

The *B.N.A. Act* granted French the status of official language alongside English but did not provide for the promotion of the French language across Canada.

2. *Manitoba: from bilingualism to unilingualism (1870 – 1989)*

In 1870, Manitoba, encompassing the former district of Assiniboa, entered the Canadian federation. Its constitution, the 1870 *Manitoba Act*, contained language provisions modelled on that of Québec. Before Manitoba became a Canadian province, the district of Assiniboa was already bilingual.

The first Manitoba legislature was "*a model of linguistic balance both in composition and procedures*"[145]. All

---

[145] See Edmund A. Aungier, *Language Legislation and*

government motions, reports or declarations were delivered by two ministers, a French-speaker and an English-speaker, each speaking in his own language. Government bills, reports, records and statutes were published in both languages.

But within a decade, due to a rapid demographic change, the Francophones were outnumbered by English-speaking settlers from Ontario. The proportion of Francophones plummeted from 55% to 16%.

In 1890, the Manitoba assembly adopted the *Official Language Act* which established English as the province's sole official language. The same year, the assembly passed the *Public Schools Act* which established a system of non-denominational

---

Official Bilingualism: the uneasy coexistence of Canada's language communities in *Canada, Confederation to Present, An interactive history of Canada*, CD-Rom, Chinook Publications (Edmonton, Alberta), 2001

schools under the supervision of a provincial advisory board. The board soon prohibited instruction in French.

The *Official Language Act* was declared unconstitutional in 1892, 1909 and 1976 by the St Boniface County Court but the Manitoba Government ignored these decisions.

In 1979 and 1985[146], the Supreme Court ruled that the Act was invalid and ordered the Manitoba government to translate the statutes and re-enact them in French.

In 1989, Manitoba opted for a compromise solution: the government would not translate all previous laws but would provide bilingual services in designated areas where there was a significant concentration of French-speakers.

---

[146] See *Re Manitoba Language Rights* (1985) & S.C.R. 721 (Can.)

3. Northwest Territories, Alberta, Saskatchewan: the forgotten bilingualism (1870 – 1989)

a) The Northwest Territories

The 1870 *Manitoba Act* provided that the lieutenant-governor[147] of Manitoba would also serve as lieutenant-governor of the Northwest territories[148]. This twinning brought government bilingualism in the

---

[147] In Canada each province is officially headed by a lieutenant-governor who represents the Crown, but true power rests in the hands of the Premier, a member of the legislature (usually the majority party leader).

[148] Formerly known as Rupert's Land and owned by the Hudson's Bay company, the Northwest Territories became part of the Dominion of Canada in 1870.

Northwest Territories. In 1875, the federal government provided the territories with their own lieutenant-governor and a capital city. Official bilingualism was established in the *Northwest Territories Act*, 1877. Like in Québec and Manitoba, English or French could be used in the legislature, in court, and the statutes as well as the records were in both languages.

Like Manitoba, the Northwest Territories were subject to a big demographic change in the following years. While at the time of the Act French-speakers constituted three quarters of the population, one decade later they only made up one fifth of it[149].

---

[149] See Edmund A. Aungier, *Language Legislation and Official Bilingualism: the uneasy coexistence of Canada's language communities* in *Canada, Confederation to Present, An interactive history of Canada*, CD-Rom, Chinook Publications (Edmonton, Alberta), 2001

The territorial government did not respect the bilingualism provisions of the Act. French versions of statutes and ordinances were published only after long delays. In 1888, Joseph Royal, the newly appointed lieutenant-governor, addressed the Northwest assembly in English and French. English-speaking legislators who were shocked to hear French spoken asked the government to put an end to bilingualism in the Territories. They sought to repeal section 110 (on bilingualism) of the *Northwest Territories Act*, 1886. A compromise proposed by the Territories' Minister of Justice was accepted in 1891: official bilingualism would be maintained for most legislative functions but the North-West Assembly would have the right to choose the language of its proceedings. In 1892 the Assembly decided that this language would be English. It also amended the *School Ordinance* that same year to make English the sole language of school instruction.

In 1894, without giving any explanation, the government of the Northwest Territories stopped to print the French version of the ordinances.

In theory the Northwest Territories are still official bilingual. In practice they are not. This issue could at any time be brought before a court like it was in the case in Saskatchewan.

b) Alberta and Saskatchewan

The provinces of Alberta and Saskatchewan were carved out of the Northwest Territories and became part of the Canadian confederation in 1905. Their constitutions perpetuated the existing laws and regulations (including official bilingualism) until such time the provincial legislature should see fit to make modifications.

The legislatures of the two provinces did not repeal the provisions for official bilingualism yet they did not resort to the French language in their proceedings. In the legislative assemblies as well as in the courts, the language used was English. It was also the only language used for the printing of provincial statutes and legislative records.

This state of things was challenged in 1981 by André Mercure before the

Saskatchewan provincial court. He requested the right to speak French in court and to receive French-language copies of the relevant provincial statutes. The court rejected his request so he went on to the Saskatchewan Court of Appeal and then to the Canadian Supreme Court.

Meanwhile an incident had taken place in Alberta's legislative assembly in 1987: opposition member Léo Piquette asked a question both in English and French to the Minister of Education. The speaker of the assembly told him to speak in English only or else he would forfeit his right to speak.

The Supreme Court ruled in the *Mercure* case the following year[150] that the provisions for official bilingualism contained in section 110 of the 1886 *Northwest Territories*

---

[150] Mercure case

Act were still valid in Saskatchewan (and therefore in Alberta too).

Following this ruling, both provinces quickly adopted legislation that rescinded section 110 but agreed to let French be spoken in legislative assemblies and courts. The new statutes (the *Languages Act* in Saskatchewan and the *Language Act* in Alberta) thus repealed official bilingualism while allowing the use of French.

4. Québec's Quiet Revolution (1960s)

During his stay in Canada in 1831, Alexis de Tocqueville sensed a strong cleavage opposing French Canadians to English Canadians. He foretold that one day French Canadians would try to set themselves free from the British.

"Although French is the language most universally spoken, the newspapers, the notices and even the shop-signs of French tradesmen are in English. Commercial undertakings are almost all in their hands. They are really the ruling class in Canada.

I doubt if this will long be so. The clergy and a great part of the not rich but enlightened classes is French, and they begin to feel their secondary position acutely. The French newspapers that I have read, put up a constant and lively opposition against the English. Up to now the people having few needs and intellectual interests, and leading, in material things, a very comfortable life, has very imperfectly glimpsed its position as a conquered nation and furnished but feeble support to the enlightened classes. But a few years ago the House of Commons, which is almost all French Canadian, has taken measures for a wide extension of education.

There is every sign that the new generation will be different from the present generation, and in a few years from now, if the English race is not prodigiously increased by emigration and does not succeed in shutting the French in the area they now occupy, the two peoples will come up against one another. I do not think that they will ever merge, or that an indissoluble union can exist between them. I still hope that the French, in spite of their conquest, will one day form a fine empire on their own in the New World, more enlightened perhaps, more moral and happier than their fathers"[151].

---

[151] See p. 187, Alexis de Tocqueville, *Journey to America*, Greenwood Press Publishers, Westport, CT., 1981

If Tocqueville's appreciation of the situation was accurate, the causes of Québec's nationalist awakening of the 1960s are old.

Prior to 1960, the Québec government played only a limited role in provincial affairs. The *Union Nationale* party which controlled the Québec government from 1944 to 1960 was rather conservative and defended the rural character of French Canada. A large proportion of the rural voters as well as the Catholic Church supported this party, headed by Premier Maurice Duplessis. But with Québec becoming a more urban and industrialised province, more and more people asked for a modernisation of the institutions which Duplessis' Government rejected. Following Duplessis' death in 1959, the Liberal Party came to power in 1960. Jean Lesage, leader of the Liberals, became Premier with the motto *"Il faut que ça change"* (Things must change). The Liberals were more in tune with the preoccupations of urban Francophones who felt that the levels of education and social services had to be improved. The Liberals were re-elected in 1962 with the slogan *"Maîtres chez nous"* (Masters in our own house)[152]. Reforms were numerous. In the field of energy, the Liberals placed the province's larger hydro-electric utilities (which had been mainly owned by English Canadians) under provincial control. French became the working language in the Hydro-Québec network and Francophones

---

[152] This slogan and idea was not supported by all political parties in Québec. There were dissensions even within the Liberal party itself. During his 1968 campaign for the leadership of the Liberal party, Quebecker Pierre Eliott Trudeau (future Prime Minister of Canada) declared « *Masters in our own house we must be, but our house is the whole of Canada* ».

soon occupied most managerial positions. Lesage also created the *Société Générale de Financement* (investment institution) to provide capital for private enterprises (this helped Francophones set up their own businesses). The government of Québec created a ministry of education in 1964 as well as regional school boards. The Catholic and Protestant Churches were not completely dismissed (as the school system continued to be divided along denominational lines) but the clergy ceded its supervisory role to the ministry of education. The government greatly increased the funding of universities and created post-secondary institutions known as CEGEPs[153].

The government also removed the Catholic Church from the area of health and

---

[153] Collège d'Enseignement Général et Professionnel : Colleges of General and Occcupational Education

social services. It took over the administration of hospitals (which was done by the Catholic Church until then) and set up the Québec Pension Plan[154]. The Separatist movement (which wanted the independence of Québec from Canada) gained momentum during this period of time which became known as the Quiet Revolution.

5. The Royal Commission on Bilingualism and Biculturalism (1963-69)

During the Quiet Revolution, the Canadian Prime Minister was the Liberal Lester Pearson. His government tried to accommodate the province by allowing it to withdraw from several federal-provincial

---

[154] The Québec Pension Plan provides for retired people, disabled people and the survivors of the deceased.

programs and by creating a Royal Commission on Bilingualism and Biculturalism. The establishment of this Commission[155] in 1963 seems to have constituted a turning point.

This commission was first called for on 20 January 1962 by André Laurendeau, editor of the Montréal Daily "*Le Devoir*". He warned that the French-Canadian malaise was a time-bomb which could have grave repercussions on the future of Canada if nothing was done on the issue of languages. The following year, Prime Minister Lester Pearson created this commission and appointed Laurendeau as well as academic Davidson Dunton to co-chair

---

[155] One should pay attention here to the choice of the word "biculturalism". At that time, few efforts were made to recognize the rights and cultures of the Aboriginals. In contrast, Section 27 of the 1982 Canadian Charter of Rights and Freedoms evokes the "*multicultural heritage of Canadians*". Biculturalism has now been replaced by multiculturalism.

it. Their mission was *"to inquire into and report upon the existing state of bilingualism and biculturalism in Canada and to recommend what steps should be taken to develop the Canadian Confederation on the basis of an equal partnership between the two founding races"*[156].

First of all, the creation of a commission dealing only with bilingualism and biculturalism was a way to recognize the importance of the two languages, but even more importantly, within a few years, the Commission realised several studies that permitted to assess the state (and needs) of bilingualism in Canada and that eventually led to the drafting of the *Official Languages Act*.

---

[156] See Edmund A. Aungier, *Language Legislation and Official Bilingualism: the uneasy coexistence of Canada's language communities* in *Canada, Confederation to Present, An interactive history of Canada*, CD-Rom, Chinook Publications (Edmonton, Alberta), 2001

In its preliminary report published in 1965, the commission concluded that *"Canada, without being fully conscious of the fact, is passing through the greatest crisis in its history"* [157] and *"the source of this crisis lies in the Province of Québec"* [158]. Many French-speaking Quebeckers were questioning their status within the confederation and claiming to be victim of cruel inequalities. In this preliminary report, the commission indicated that there was a conflict opposing a French-

---

[157] See Edmund A. Aungier, *Language Legislation and Official Bilingualism: the uneasy coexistence of Canada's language communities* in *Canada, Confederation to Present, An interactive history of Canada*, CD-Rom, Chinook Publications (Edmonton, Alberta), 2001

[158] More precisely the commission focused on the basis of the Canadian confederation: the *B.N.A. Act*. *"(I)t would appear from what is happening that the state of affairs established in 1867, and never seriously challenged, is now for the first time being rejected by the French Canadians of Quebec"*.

speaking majority inside Quebec, and an English-speaking majority outside Quebec. The commission acknowledged the fact that Quebec was a "distinct society"[159].

In five years of studies, the commission painted a clear picture of the state of bilingualism in contemporary Canada. The results of the research were striking:
Canadian public service was mainly English-speaking and required French-speaking employees to have a working knowledge of English. French speakers were under-represented in management and professional positions. In the private sector in the province of Québec the language of work was generally English (except for blue-collar workers).

---

[159] This expression was coined by Québec's Prime Minister Jean Lesage in reference to Québec's unique civil code, education system, and political institutions.

Various provinces had adopted measures to eliminate the official status of the French language. Québec was the only province which provided a set of schools for its official-language minority, while nothing equivalent was available for French speakers in the English-speaking provinces.

The commission made recommendations directed both to the federal and provincial governments. The main recommendation was to make a formal declaration that English and French would be Canada's official languages, not only in parliament and the courts but also in the federal administration (in order to ensure bilingualism in the workplace the commission recommended the creation of French-language units). This bilingualism was to be enshrined in a specific statute on official languages and monitored by an ombudsman, the commissioner of official languages.

The commission also proposed that French-language services be available not only in Québec but also in the national capital and elsewhere in districts where the French-speakers made up at least 10% of the population (the same was proposed for English speakers living in Québec districts where they constituted at least 10% of the population).

The commission rejected the idea of establishing unilingual territories (in other words a province – Québec – whose sole language would be French and the rest of Canada whose sole language would be English). This option would have been simpler to implement but at the expense of linguistic minorities.

The commission also recommended that the provinces of Ontario and New Brunswick (home to the largest French-speaking communities) become officially bilingual.

6. The Official Languages Act: official bilingualism becomes a reality in practice (1969)

In 1969, following the work of the Commission, the *Official Languages Act* was proposed to Parliament and passed. Its section two read that *"The English and French languages are the official languages of Canada for all purposes of the Parliament and Government of Canada, and possess and enjoy equality of status and equal rights and privileges as to their use in all the institutions of the Parliament and Government of Canada"*.

It had three main aims:

the equality of English and French in Parliament, within the Government of Canada, the federal administration and the institutions mentioned in the Act;

the preservation and development of English and French language communities in Canada;

the equality of English and French in Canadian society.

The same year, New Brunswick enacted a similar statute, also called *Official Languages Act*, and became Canada's first and only bilingual province. Ontario did not follow the commission's recommendation and remained officially unilingual.

The clear difference between the *Official Languages Act* and the *B.N.A. Act* was that the former contained pro-active provisions designed not only to guarantee the right to use the two languages but to ensure that bilingualism would be a reality.

It is Prime Minister Pierre Eliott Trudeau who introduced the *Official Languages Act*. Trudeau worked to promote a pan-Canadian nationalism, the commission's comments on Québec's distinct character were therefore nowhere to be found in the Act.

Bilingualism was supported by the Trudeau government but biculturalism was not. Instead the government launched a policy of multiculturalism which valued the legacy of all the peoples that formed Canada (including also Aboriginals, non-French and non-British immigrants).

Following the bilingualism policy, other statutes and regulations were passed in various fields, including the *Consumer Packaging and Labelling Act*[160] (1974) which provided for bilingual packaging throughout the country.

---

[160] The *Consumer Packaging and Labelling Act* required the use of both English and French on all consumer packaging across the country. This Act, whose purpose might seem negligible was nonetheless one of the most visible embodiments of the bilingualism policy. Indeed, customers all across the country were reminded of the bilingual nature of the state and its detractors used it as an example of the costs of bilingualism policy. – *"This was the point where the reality of official bilingualism hit home for many English-speaking Canadians, as airline attendants gave emergency instructions in both official languages and children honed their French skills by reading the back of a Cornflakes box."*, in *History of Canadian Language Politics*, Mapleleafweb.com (Department of Political Science, University of Lethbridge, Canada).

7. Resistance in Québec: the Charter of the French Language (1977)

This federal bilingualism policy was challenged both in Québec and before the courts.

In Québec, the 1977 *Charter of the French Language* (also known as *Bill 101*) banned the use of all languages except French on commercial signs in the province[161]

---

[161] The provisions of the *Charter* were very restrictive but the ban of other languages was not total as bilingual or multilingual signs (featuring French) were allowed inside public or commercial buildings (such as municipal buildings in places with a majority of English-speakers, schools, health services, social services, small companies with less than 4 employees). Moreover, unilingualism (with a language other than French) was also allowed for religious, political, humanitarian or ideological messages. – It is also interesting to note that *"(i)n practice, the (1977 Charter of the French Language) has been applied with a great deal of tolerance.*

(directly attacking the aforementioned *Consumer Packaging and Labelling Act*). It also required children of immigrants residing in Québec to attend French-language public schools[162].

In the 1988 *Ford v. Québec* case, the Supreme Court ruled that the commercial sign law provisions of the *Charter of the French*

The commercial signs in English (unilingual or bilingual) have always been commonplace in the Metropolis (Montréal), particularly in West Island where there is a concentration of Anglophones; it was moreover frequent to come across signs that did not comply with the (Charter) in the region of Québec (...). In the cities of Pierrefonds, Roxboro, Pointe-Claire, Baie d'Urfé, Kirkland, Beaconsfield and Saint-Laurent, several businesses have only-English signs (...). Finally provincial law does not apply to federal bodies which have to put signs featuring the two official languages of the federal government". – See p. 157, Jacques Leclerc, *La guerre des langues dans l'affichage*, vlb éditeur

[162] The children of Canadian citizens who had received their education in Canada in English could attend English-language public schools.

Language banning the use of outdoor signs in English were unconstitutional. The Court ruled that Québec had the right to impose French but could not forbid English. Indeed the *Canadian Charter of Rights and Freedoms* guarantees freedom of speech[163] and this applies in the commercial field as well.

The Québec national assembly tried to resist. In 1989, it invoked the *notwithstanding* clause of the Canadian constitution to set aside the enforcement of the ruling for five years. Meanwhile a U.N. appeal of the *McIntyre* case[164] resulted in a condemnation of Québec's sign law and thus reinforced the position of the Canadian Supreme Court.

Québec's assembly eventually had to give in and amend the *Charter*. It did so

---

[163] Cf. *Canadian Charter of Rights and Freedoms*, Section 2 b): *"Everyone has the following fundamental freedoms: (...) freedom of thought, belief, opinion and expression..."*

[164] McIntyre and others v. Canada

through its *Bill 86* passed in 1993 which allowed other languages on commercial signs as long as French would be markedly predominant (as suggested by the Supreme Court in its decision).

In 2005 it is the provisions on Québec's language of instruction that were reviewed by the Supreme Court. It found the limiting of access to English-language public education in breach of the *Canadian Charter of Rights and Freedoms*. The Court laid out a set of criteria to bring Québec's law in conformity with the *Canadian Charter of Rights and Freedoms*.

While its attempts to challenge the official bilingualism policy were unsuccessful, Québec has managed to gain a form of leeway. The strength of nationalism and the big support for independence are a sword of Damocles hanging above Canadian unity.

The Supreme Court's stance in the aforementioned cases illustrates this concern. It was firm but at the same time constructive. The Court proposed solutions that would enable Québec to protect its particularities while remaining consistent with the Canadian constitution.

A new *Official Languages Act* was adopted by Parliament in 1988. It repeated and qualified the obligations under the *Canadian Charter of Rights and Freedoms*.

8. The Canadian Charter of Rights and Freedoms (1982)

The Canadian constitution is not one document but several. The aforementioned *B.N.A. Act* is the first one, the 1982 *Canadian Charter of Rights and Freedoms* is another one.

The *Canadian Charter of Rights and Freedoms* contains provisions on bilingualism and official language rights (sections 16 to 23). The Charter declares English and French to be official languages of Canada with equal status. It also declares both languages as official languages of New Brunswick.

9. The Second Official Languages Act (1988)

In a survey on law and languages in Canada made for the Royal Commission on Bilingualism and Biculturalism, Claude-Armand Sheppard[165] pointed out the practical and judicial difficulties resulting from legal bilingualism, as well as the inequalities and their causes. Overall, Sheppard noted that the setting up of a truly fully bilingual legal system was feasible but that it would cost money, time and require more bilingual people trained in law. It seems that these comments made in 1971 were still relevant two decades later.

---

[165] See Claude-Armand Sheppard, *The Law of Languages in Canada*, Studies of the Royal Commission on Bilingualism and Biculturalism, Information Canada (Ottawa), 1971, 414 p.

In 1988 a second *Official Languages Act* was passed (and repealed the first one). It was much more comprehensive than the first version (it had 111 sections rather than 41 in the first version). The second version clarified and expanded the requirements for official-language use in federal institutions including the legislative, executive and judicial branches. The commissioner of official languages was given new powers to enforce the Act, including the right to seek a remedy before courts.

The *Criminal Code* was also amended to allow the use of both languages in criminal cases in any court in Canada.

a) A bigger role for the Commissioner of Official Languages

A clear pro-active attitude can be felt in the Official Languages Act: both official languages are to be protected and promoted. The Act does not only provide for bilingualism of the law and communication with the federal institutions in English and French, it contains provisions on languages of work in the federal institutions (in Canada and abroad)[166], provisions on equal employment opportunities in federal institutions for speakers of both languages[167] and provisions on the advancement of both languages (in fact the promotion of bilingualism)[168].

---

[166] Cf. Section 34: *"English and French are the languages of work in all federal institutions, and officers and employees of all federal institutions have the right to use either official language…"*

[167] Cf. Part VI, Sections 39 & 40.

[168] Cf. Part VII, Section 41: *"The Government of Canada is committed to*

(a) enhancing the vitality of the English and French linguistic minority communities in Canada and supporting

The Act also developed the powers of the Commissioner of Official Languages[169] whose duty is *"to take all actions and measures (...) with a view to ensuring recognition of the status of each of the official languages and compliance with the spirit and intent of this Act"*[170]. The duty of the Commissioner is also *"to conduct and carry out investigations either on his own initiative or pursuant to any complaint made to (him/her) and to report and make recommendations"*[171].

Seeing his/her legitimacy increase with the language provisions of the *Canadian*

and assisting their development; and

(b) fostering the full recognition and use of both English and French in Canadian society."

See also Sections 42 to 45.

[169] See *Official Languages Act*, Part IX: *"Commissioner of Official Languages"*, Sections 49 to 75.

[170] See *Official Languages Act*, Part IX, Section 56(1)

[171] See *Official Languages Act*, Part IX, Section 56(2)

Charter of Rights and Freedoms as well as the new *Official Languages Act*, the Commissioner has been more and more active in the past years. In 2000, the Commissioner denounced the federal government's *"persistent inertia"*[172] in implementing the Act. She also announced that her office would expand its role: its agents would not only investigate complaints but also work to make bilingualism a priority within the public service and the federal administration.

The federal government reacted to the Commissioner's criticisms. In 2002 the Throne speech included commitments to promote Canada's linguistic diversity. In March 2003 the Government released an Action Plan for

---

[172] See *Commissioner of Official Languages Annual Report 1999-2000* (http://www.ocol-clo.gc.ca/archives/ar_ra/1999_00/1999_00-toc_tdm_e.htm)

Official Languages. In its preface, Prime Minister Chretien presented bilingualism as an advantage for Canada: *"Our linguistic duality means better access to markets and more jobs and greater mobility for workers"*[173]. This Action Plan contained provisions in three main fields: development of bilingual education, community services for Francophone and Anglophone minorities, promotion of both languages in the federal public service.

---

[173] Cited in *Canada's new commitment to official bilingualism*, Mapleleaweb.com (Department of Political Science, University of Lethbridge, Canada)

b) Entrenchment of bilingualism in the National Capital Region

Ottawa became the capital of Canada in 1857. At the time, the country was only composed of two provinces: Ontario and Quebec. Ottawa was chosen because of its advantageous location: on the border of the two provinces and far enough from the United States not to be an easy target for the American army. Ottawa is in fact in the province of Ontario. The city was built on the southern bank on the Ottawa river which is a natural border between Ontario and Quebec.

The Government, the Parliament, the Supreme Court and many other federal institutions are based in Ottawa. The growth of the city[174] over the years led to the

---

[174] *"Ottawa was perhaps the most impressive creation of Canada's first hundred years. The little town of*

constitution of the National Capital Region (N.C.R.). Unlike Washington D.C., Ottawa has not been made a separate district under federal control. The N.C.R. is a zone which includes government agencies, parks, and tourist sites in Ottawa and surrounding municipalities.

1867, cowering like an overgrown lumber camp at the edge of the pine forest, had become a large city of close to 500,000 people. (...) For many years, new buildings were added slowly, one by one, and at long intervals; but the coming of the welfare and interventionist state, whose permanency was clinched by the Second World War, vastly enlarged the sphere of government; and, from then on, building construction hardly ever ceased its struggle to keep up with the insatiable demands of constantly increasing masses of civil servants for office space and houses. The original Victorian small town (...) was now surrounded, on three sides, by a new and populous city (...). On its fourth side, across the Ottawa river in Quebec, was the town of Hull (...), which had gradually become a dormitory suburb for many French-Canadian civil servants", See p. 350-351, Donald Creighton, *Canada's first century*, MacMillan (Toronto, 1970).

The second version of the *Official Languages Act* contains provisions specifically aimed at the N.C.R. Pursuant to the act, federal institutions located in the N.C.R. must ensure that the work environment is conducive to the effective use of both official languages[175]. The federal institutions based in the N.C.R. also have the duty to make services and work instruments available to their employees in both languages[176]. They must also ensure that regularly and widely used automated systems for the processing and communication of data can be used in either official language[177]. In these institutions, supervisors must be able to communicate in both official languages and any management group that is responsible for the general

---

[175] Cf. *Official Languages Act*, subsection 35(1)(a).

[176] Cf. *Official Languages Act*, subsection 36(1)(a).

[177] Cf. *Official Languages Act*, subsection 36(1)(b).

direction of the institution as a whole must have the capacity to function in both official languages[178]. In other words, the act entrenched but also fortified Ottawa's bilingualism.

Since all the main federal institutions are based in Ottawa, the provisions of the *Official Languages Act* concerning the N.C.R. result in a fundamentally bilingual civil service. The provisions apply to the core of all the key institutions[179] and ensure that their personnel works in both official languages.

10. The incomplete recognition of Aboriginal peoples' rights

---

[178] Cf. *Official Languages Act*, subsection 36(1)(c).

[179] Most federal institutions have their headquarters in Ottawa. Therefore the managers of the headquarters must all be bilingual.

According to the 2001 census, 1.3 million Canadians claim to have Aboriginal ancestry[180]. This represents 3.3% of the whole Canadian population. After long years of discrimination and ostracism, Aboriginals finally saw their rights effectively recognised in the second half of the 20th century… but their languages were not granted any special protection.

a) A special status for Aboriginals

When the English and the French set up colonies in the different parts of what is now Canada, they usually signed treaties with the local Aboriginals. These treaties granted the locals rights and privileges (e.g. the right to fish or hunt in certain areas) in exchange for a

---

[180] See 2001 census

transfer of authority over what used to be "their"[181] lands. These rights were confirmed by subsequent major pieces of legislation such as the 1763 Royal Proclamation, the 1867 British North America Act and the 1982 Constitution Act[182].

Until 1982 many of these rights seemed to have become rather theoretical. The

---

[181] The concept of land ownership was alien to the Native peoples. The idea that land could be bought did not make sense from an Aboriginal cultural and spiritual perspective. Aboriginals considered themselves the spiritual guardians of the land, not its owners. Land was seen as a gift from the Great Spirit and its resources were to be used for survival purposes only. The concept of "surrendering" land created confusion in the Aboriginal communities and might have (mis)lead them to sign treaties without fully realising the consequences. – See Canada in the Making website (http://www.canadiana.org).

[182] The 1867 British North America Act (BNA Act) is now also known as the Constitution Act. In order not to confuse it with the 1982 Constitution Act, it will be referred to as BNA Act in this dissertation.

Constitution gave them a long awaited recognition. Section 35 of the Constitution states that *"the existing Aboriginal and treaty rights of the Aboriginal peoples of Canada are hereby recognized and affirmed"*. The constitutionalisation of these rights has rendered them virtually inextinguishable[183]. They are also protected from potential interference with other fundamental rights by section 25 of the Canadian Charter of Rights and Freedoms which provides that *"The guarantee in this Charter of certain rights and freedoms shall not be construed so as to abrogate or derogate from any aboriginal treaty or other rights or freedoms that pertain to the aboriginal peoples of Canada"*.

---

[183] The precedents pieces of legislation which guaranteed these rights could indeed be repealed by the English parliament.

The essence of the rights protected by the constitution and the charter is still somewhat vague. Many of the claims that could be made by Aboriginals are intrinsically hard to establish[184]. Yet, these provisions have first and foremost an important symbolic meaning. The recognition of the Aboriginals' rights was an affirmation of their place among the people of Canada. Section 27 of the Charter – vague as well - also goes in this direction: *"This Charter shall be interpreted in a manner consistent with the preservation and enhancement of the multicultural heritage of Canadians"*. Canada is thus not a bicultural country but a multicultural country and each part of its heritage is valued. As Canadian Chief Justice Beverley McLachlin explained, "*legal processes, while not the only or even*

---

[184] See Chapter four, 2), 2.1.2, "*Let us face it, we are all here to stay*"

the most important way of healing the post-colonial rifts between Aboriginal and non-Aboriginal peoples, play an important role" [185]. The main focus of contemporary Canadian law dealing with Aboriginals therefore seems to be to repair the injustices of the past. *"(T)he law secures for us a space in which we all can carry out the conversations that will help us to work out the accommodations to permit us to live together in peace for the future - in short reconciliation"*[186].

Canadian Aboriginals are given a special status by several other pieces of federal

---

[185] See Beverley McLachlin, *Aboriginal Peoples and Reconciliation*, 9 Canterbury L. Rev., 240 at 246 (2003). – In his reasons in the *Delgamuukw* case, Chief Justice Lamer concluded *"Let us face it, we are all here to stay"*, *Delgamuukw v. British Columbia*, (1997) 3 SCR 1010, para 186.

[186] See Beverley McLachlin, *Aboriginal Peoples and Reconciliation*, 9 Canterbury L. Rev., 240 at 247 (2003).

legislation. The Canadian *Criminal Code*, provides for instance that Aboriginal background must be considered in certain sentencing contexts[187]. Sentencing practices can now also include sentencing circles in which the community participates and where the emphasis is on restoring the harmony between the Aboriginal offender and the community[188].

These provisions and systems linked to policies of affirmative action are an attempt to turn tables. Several decades ago, the Indian Act[189], while granting several rights to aboriginals, also put lots of constraints on

---

[187] Canadian Criminal Code, s. 718.2(e): *"All available sanctions other than imprisonment that are reasonable in the circumstances should be considered for all offenders, with particular attention to the circumstances of aboriginal offenders"*.

[188] See www.usask.ca/nativelaw/publications/scircle.htm

[189] Reference : date & content of the act

them[190]. The Canadian Supreme Court already started to act on this in the 1970s with the landmark case *Drybones*[191] by stating that provisions of the Indian Act that were inconsistent with the principle of equality before the law could not be applied. Section 15 of the Canadian Charter of Rights and Freedoms guarantees *"equality before and under law and equal protection and benefit of law"* (s. 15.1) while at the same time authorising affirmative action programs: *"any law, program or activity that has as its object the amelioration of conditions of disadvantaged individuals or groups"* is not precluded by the article (s. 15.2). A different

---

[190] They had rights but not the same rights as the "white" Canadians.

[191] 1970 SCR 282 – Several provisions of the Indian Act made it an offence for aboriginals to be intoxicated off the reserves. The Supreme Court held that these provisions contravened with the guarantee of equality before the law.

treatment can therefore lawfully exist but it needs to be in favour of the disadvantaged Aboriginals, not a restraint upon rights that all other Canadians could enjoy.

b) The absence of language rights

All these elements show a clear will to recognise the Aboriginals' rights and their identities. For Chief Justice McLachlin, *"(t)he law is not concerned only with the issues of Aboriginal entitlements arising from history. The law is also concerned with the contemporary problems of Aboriginal peoples, as they struggle with the fragmentation and dislocation of their bi-cultural identities"*[192]. Yet no language rights have been granted to

---

[192] See Beverley McLachlin, *Aboriginal Peoples and Reconciliation*, 9 Canterbury L. Rev., 240 at 246 (2003).

help Aboriginals prevent this dislocation. Their special status does not include a right to have access to public service (or the publication of the law) in their languages. Except in the province of Nunavut (which has a small - mainly Inuit - population[193]) Aboriginal languages have not been given recognition and many of them are becoming extinct.

Arguably, the protection granted to the Aboriginal heritage could be considered paradoxical. Indeed while fishing or hunting rights granted in the 17th or 18th centuries are fiercely protected[194] (although most Aboriginals would nowadays buy their food at the local grocery store) Aboriginal languages are left without any kind of protection.

---

[193] It is important to underline the fact that Nunavut has only 28.700 inhabitants (2002 census) while hundreds of thousands of Aboriginals are scattered across Canada.

[194] See below the Supreme Court on Aboriginal rights

The only "language right" available to Canadian aboriginals is that of having the assistance of an interpreter for judiciary proceedings[195]. A right which is not granted to Aboriginals in particular but to anyone party to proceedings who does not understand the language in which they are conducted.

Several other legal provisions deal with Aboriginal languages and while not granting them increased protection provide that Canada's language policies and regulations should not contravene with their preservation.

A good example is section 7 (3) of the 1985 Official Languages Act. Section 7 (1) of

---

[195] S. 14, Canadian Charter of Rights and Freedoms: *"A party or witness in any proceedings who does not understand or speak the language in which the proceedings are conducted or who is deaf has the right to the assistance of an interpreter"*.

the Act provides that *"any instrument made in the execution of a legislative power conferred by or under an Act of Parliament (...) shall be made (...) printed and published in both official languages"*. But subsection 7 (3) specifies that subsection 7 (1) does not apply to laws, by-laws or other instruments established by an Indian band, band council in order *"to perform a governmental function in relation to an Indian band or other group of aboriginal people"*. In other words, subsection 7 (3) of the Official Languages Act does not impose on Aboriginal institutions the obligation of bilingualism which is imposed on other Canadian institutions.

Another example is section 83 of the Official Languages Act. Subsection 83 (1) provides that *"(n)othing in this Act abrogates or derogates from any legal or customary right acquired or enjoyed either before or after the coming into force of this Act with respect to any language that is not English or French"*. This provision echoes section 35 of the Constitution Act which recognizes the existing treaty rights of Aboriginals. Subsection 83 (2) provides that *"nothing in this Act shall be interpreted in a manner that is inconsistent with the preservation and enhancement of languages other than English or French"*. Here again a very vague phrasing which could apply not only to Aboriginal languages but also to other languages spoken in Canada[196]. Aboriginal language protection by the federal state is therefore rather passive than active.

---

[196] The ten most spoken languages in Canada are: English (17,352,315 speakers), French (7,703,325), Chinese (853,745), Italian (469,485), German (438,080), Punjabi (271,220), Spanish (245,500), Portuguese (213,815), Polish (208,375), Arabic (199,940). The most spoken Aboriginal languages are Inukltitut (29,005) and Ojibway (21,000). – Source: Statistics Canada, 2001

While it is believed essential to teach French to people who live in British Columbia it is not deemed equally important to revive Aboriginal languages.

Even if there was a political will to promote these languages, there would be intrinsic obstacles. As a matter of fact, Aboriginal languages are numerous (fifty) and spoken by a very small number of people[197]. Moreover in a 1996 census 67.8% of Aboriginal people reported to be native English speakers. Interestingly, in the same census, 47% of Aboriginal people residing in the province of Québec reported an Aboriginal language as their mother tongue (which was the highest proportion in the country[198]).

---

[197] Cf. note 125

[198] The territory of Nunavut had not been created yet.

V. LEGISLATION AND LANGUAGE

1. General considerations on bilingual legislation

A short overview of the processes necessary to the creation of bilingual legislation shows that it is easier to write about it than to actually make it. Draftsmanship (a) is in itself a complex issue. Several methods for producing bilingual legislation all have their advantages and disadvantages. In the phrasing of the law (b) drafters must also take into account the nature of English and French, as well as each language's legislative style. Finally, material constraints (c) often come in the way.

a) The question of draftsmanship

The requirement of legal bilingualism brings about the question of draftsmanship. In order for statutes to be available in two languages they need to be either drafted in both languages at the same time, or to be drafted in one language and then translated. Quality and equality are here completely interdependent: if one version of a statute is poorly written or too obscure, it will not be relied on. True legal bilingualism cannot exist if one version of the law exists only as a reference document while the other one is (*de jure* or *de facto*) the official one.

To consider and analyse the truthfulness of two versions of a law one can look at them vertically and horizontally. If the two versions say the same thing when read as a whole, they can be said to have achieved vertical equality. Yet even so one version might have more clauses than the other or present things in different places. When the two versions say the same thing in the same place, they can be said to have achieved horizontal equality. Horizontal equality facilitates comparison between the two texts[199].

The two versions of a good bilingual law should therefore be equal vertically and horizontally. Independently of the authoring process chosen to produce bilingual laws, the vertical and horizontal equality are important criteria: the more equal the two versions, the

---

[199] Chief Legislative Counsel of Ontario Donald L. Revell developed this theory. Being in charge of supervising the production of bilingual laws in Ontario, he uses the vertical-horizontal equality criteria to determine assess quality. – See p. 36, Donald L. Revell, *Bilingual Legislation: The Ontario Experience*, Statute Law Review, Volume 19, Number 1, pp. 32-40, 1998.

smaller the chances that they would be interpreted in different ways[200].

(1) Unilingual drafting and translation

aa) Subsequent translation

The most common method to make bilingual statutes is to first draft them in one language and have them translated later. This is how Canadian bilingual laws were made until the 1969 *Official Languages Act*. Until that time, there was no simultaneous bilingual drafting in Canada. The subsequent translation method has several advantages. Firstly it does not change or slow down the

---

[200] Two versions of a statute could indeed be interpreted in different ways just because of the location of material in the text.

classic unilingual drafting process, and secondly it costs less money and time than all the other methods. The disadvantage, which cannot be minimized, is a usually poorer quality of translation.

The draftsman of a statute must first of all understand the legislative policy which the statute is intended to express. Her/his task is to familiarize her/himself with the subject-matter, as well as with the legislative problems involved and the proposed solutions. In cases where several government departments could be interested in a piece of legislation, the draftsman might even need to bring together officials from these various departments. It is only after achieving thorough understanding of these aspects that s/he can start drafting the bill. At the drafting stage, the draftsman has normally become imbued with the spirit in which the original policy and the subsequent modifications were conceived. In contrast, the translator only reads the finished product without having a deep knowledge of the context.

The translator who has not participated in the drafting has been deprived of the opportunity to familiarize her/himself with the true intention and purpose of the legislator. S/he is therefore at disadvantage when trying to convey the legislator's intentions in another language.

Legal translation requires the same skills as literary translation but it does not require the same expertise. Indeed, in order to translate the law, one needs to understand its intricacies in both languages and also – in the case of Canada – in both the civil law and the common law traditions. The same term is sometimes used in these two traditions to denote different legal institutions or, conversely, different words are sometimes used to describe essentially identical notions. These linguistic pitfalls make information on the "spirit" of the statute all the more vital to a good translation[201].

---

[201] *"Translation is not and can never be a purely mechanical process which can be undertaken by anyone with a working knowledge of both languages. It must, if it is to be effective, be a paraphrase which takes account of idiom as well as syntax. The professional translator of informational material must have a broad cultural background to enable him to reach beyond comparable idiom and seek equivalent image. To arrive at the best equivalent of a particular slogan or forceful metaphor may take as many hours as several hundred words of routine translation. Scientific and technical material presents problems that take longer to solve than those of an ordinary text.*

In Canada, translation between English and French presents peculiar problems. In each language many words have acquired connotations unknown in the country of origin. French in Canada has absorbed different anglicisms from those adopted in France, as well as many American

Moreover, since the translator did not take part to the drafting s/he will not have had any opportunity to ask for precisions or suggest changes in the draft which could have helped make both versions more alike and avoid polysemous terms.

Until 1969, all statutes were translated by the Federal Translation Bureau, which is not a part of the department of Justice. Created in 1934, the Bureau was meant to provide translation for federal bodies. It received (and still receives) many assignments from government departments other than

words and terms, and no good French-American dictionary is available. English usage in Canada has accepted American meanings of some words but adheres to the British meanings of others." Report of the Royal Commission on Government Organization, cited p. 113 in p. 151, Claude-Armand Sheppard, *The Law of Languages in Canada*, Studies of the Royal Commission on Bilingualism and Biculturalism, Information Canada (Ottawa, 1971).

that of Justice. Before 1969, its staff did not comprise any specialists in the fields covered by individual statutes[202]. Moreover, being detached from the Parliament or department of Justice, its staff could not rely on the assistance of experts in the particular fields under consideration.

Bills were first drafted in English and then translated without any interaction between the translator and the drafter[203]. In

---

[202] At that time, there was a shortage of trained translators. Applicants for employment with the Bureau were asked to have either a university degree or two years' experience in translation or language teaching. The selection process consisted in oral and written examinations in translation. – See p. 114, Claude-Armand Sheppard, *The Law of Languages in Canada*, Studies of the Royal Commission on Bilingualism and Biculturalism, Information Canada, Ottawa, 1971

[203] *"It would have been impossible to have achieved the political bargain that led to the creation of Canada in 1867 unless the French culture of Québec had been recognized in the Constitution Act, 1867. This Act provided*

his report to the Royal Commission on Bilingualism and Biculturalism, Claude-Armand Sheppard denounced this translation method as a clear obstacle to real legal bilingualism. *"Federal statutes are not badly drafted English laws but poorly translated English laws. Anyone who has examined the French text of any federal statute, even in the most perfunctory manner, has become painfully aware not so much of grammatical*

---

for official bilingualism at the federal level and in Québec. However, it was not until the 1960s and what was known as the "Quiet Revolution" in Québec, that the federal government took legal bilingualism very seriously. From what I have been told by a former Chief Legislative Counsel for Canada, drafting was done in English in Ottawa. The text was shipped for translation to another department a few miles away in Hull, Québec. There was virtually no contact between drafters and translators. There were countless discrepancies between the English and French texts.", See p. 1100, Donald L. Revell, *Authoring bilingual laws: the importance of process*, Brook. J. Int'l. L. Vol. 29:3 2004, pp. 1085-1105.

errors as of the totally non-Latin and non-idiomatic use of language. In fact, the French text is frequently almost incomprehensible to a French lawyer"[204].

bb) Participatory translation

Instead of having the translator discover the law once it is drafted, it is also possible to associate the translator to the drafting process. The translator's presence during the drafting would allow her/him to get acquainted with the subject-matter, ask questions and propose other formulations.

The subsequent translation method has several disadvantages which can be solved by

---

[204] See p. 114, Claude-Armand Sheppard, *The Law of Languages in Canada*, Studies of the Royal Commission on Bilingualism and Biculturalism, Information Canada, Ottawa, 1971, 414 p.

having the translator participate to the drafting. This option also has a major disadvantage: its cost. Indeed, the time that the translator spends observing the drafting s/he could spend translating other documents. This option costs therefore more time and money than subsequent translation.

Most unilingual provinces that publish some bilingual legislation tend to use a method which leans towards participatory translation: translators are not always associated to the drafting process but they are usually encouraged to have a thorough dialogue with the drafter.

(2) Bilingual drafting

Equality of languages implies that a language should be given precedence over the other. Federal institutions and the province of New Brunswick use co-drafting since the implementation of the official languages policy. Apart from quality, this method guarantees equality, which is a key political issue in a bilingual context. When the two versions are drafted in parallel, none can be granted precedence over the other. In contrast, in the case of unilingual drafting followed by translation, judges faced with versions would rather look for the legislator's intent in the original[205] than in the translation.

Double drafting, another method of bilingual drafting which resembles co-drafting, has been tested but not retained.

---

[205] See below: III, D, 2, b), (3) The method of interpretation of statutes

aa) Co-drafting

Co-drafting is used by the federal government and by the province of New Brunswick. Its functioning is simple: Two drafters (one English-mother-tongue and one French-mother-tongue) are assigned to each project. Each receives instructions from the client (usually a government department). One of them acts as the lead drafter and prepares the first draft. The other waits until the first draft is finished before preparing her/his version. The second drafter discusses with the lead drafter any potential problems found in the first draft. This dialogue continues until the final versions of the two drafts are ready.

The object of co-drafting is to produce two idiomatic versions of the same law. This method ensures that each text is a true original. English and French cultural groups are treated with full equality because neither version can be considered to have an inferior status. While co-drafting usually costs more than drafting followed by translation, it brings an equality (which many Canadians desire and) which cannot be brought any other method.

bb) Double drafting

Another form of bilingual drafting is the double drafting. Here there is a single bilingual drafter who prepares both versions of a bill. While co-drafting involves two personalities (and therefore two sensitivities, two ways to express oneself), the advantage of double drafting is that the same person authors the two versions. The disadvantage is the absence of dialogue and proof-reading. It could also be assumed that in some cases drafters would first write the bill in the language they feel more comfortable with and then proceed to a mere translation of their own work. Moreover, having one person draft the two versions of a bill might be cheaper than co-drafting but it also usually takes more time. Finally, double drafting – however advantageous or appropriate it may seem – is difficult to set up because there are few people who have the required skills (lawyers fully fluent in the two languages and knowing the intricacies of the civil law and common law traditions).

This method is not used much in Canada. One example of its use is for exceptional cases in Ontario[206] when the

---

[206] See p. 36-37, Donald L. Revell, *Bilingual Legislation: The Ontario Experience*, Statute Law Review,

amount of work needed is minimal or when the translation section of the Office of Legislative Counsel is working to its full capacity.

b) The question of phrasing

Canada's two official languages are not identical in structure and do not always have equivalents for all terminology. Some concepts can be explained more simply in one language than in the other. Producing equivalent versions of the same laws is therefore intrinsically challenging. Whether the method used is drafting followed by translation or bilingual drafting, the risk of ambiguity is the same. It lies in what anyone can hardly depart from: the nature of the languages[207].

---

[207] As legal comparatist Nicholas Kasirer pointed out, *"on should expect a certain relation of dependence (or even interdependence) to exist between legal ideas and the language used to 'translate/express' them"*. The French verb used by N. Kasirer is "traduire" which, in the context of this sentence means both "translate" and "express". It seems that the very translation of this sentence epitomizes in itself the point made by the author. – See Nicholas Kasirer, *Dire ou définir le droit?*, 28 R.J.T. n.s. 143 at 175, 1994

(1) Steering clear from le double entendre

In an article on bilingual legislation[208], Michael J.B. Wood, Bilingual Legislative Counsel in Ontario, gave several concrete examples to illustrate this question.

As explained before, some concepts of one language have no equivalent in the other. Some ideas have specific connotations in English and other connotations in French. In addition to this English and French have a fair share of structural linguistic differences. The very way sentences are built is different, two distinct constructions might thus be needed in order to express the same idea in the two languages. The more the two versions of a

[208] See Michael J.B. Wood, *Drafting Bilingual Legislation in Canada: Examples of Beneficial Cross-Pollination Between the Two Language Versions*, Statute Law Review, Volume 17, Number 1, pp. 66-77, 1996.

statutes differ (be in their content or in the way the contents are organised) the greater the risk of misunderstanding.

The word *any*, for instance, which is used very commonly in statutes does not have an equivalent in French. It therefore risks being misunderstood and mistranslated.

The following sentence can be translated in French in two different ways (with two different meanings):

The report shall include <u>any</u> document specified in the schedule.

1) Le rapport comprend l'un des documents énoncés à l'annexe. (lit. : *the report shall include <u>one of the</u> documents specified in the schedule*).

2) Le rapport comprend les documents énoncés à l'annexe. (lit. : *the report*

shall include <u>all the</u> documents specified in the schedule).

For more clarity the drafter should refrain from using any and rather use "the" or "all" depending on the intended meaning of the sentence[209].

Pronominal phrases (such as *thereof*) which are often used in statutes have no equivalent in French and can therefore easily be misinterpreted. The following sentence illustrates this ambiguity:

The Minister may grant an exemption to a town or a village or a part <u>thereof</u>.

1) Le ministre peut accorder une exemption à une ville ou un village ou

---

[209] Example cited by Michael J.B. Wood, p. 70 in *Drafting Bilingual Legislation in Canada: Examples of Beneficial Cross-Pollination Between the Two Language Versions*, Statute Law Review, Volume 17, Number 1, pp. 66-77, 1996.

une partie <u>de l'un de ceux-ci</u>. (lit. : *The Minister may grant an exemption to a town or a village or a part <u>of either of them</u>*).

2) Le ministre peut accorder une exemption à une ville ou un village ou une partie <u>de celui-ci</u>. (lit. : *The Minister may grant an exemption to a town or a village or a part <u>of a village</u>*). [210]

Chains of qualifiers[211], typical of Germanic languages, are commonplace in English. French language does not allow these chains and uses modifying phrases instead. These

---

[210] Example cited by Michael J.B. Wood, p. 70 in *Drafting Bilingual Legislation in Canada: Examples of Beneficial Cross-Pollination Between the Two Language Versions*, Statute Law Review, Volume 17, Number 1, pp. 66-77, 1996.

[211] Chains of qualifiers are nouns and adjectives placed together in a chain.

chains are often resorted to for their compactness, but they can make French translation quite complicated.

Section 23(b) of the *Canadian Charter of Rights and Freedoms* contains a chain of qualifiers. This section provides that the right of Canadians to have their children receive primary and secondary school instruction in the language of the English or French linguistic minority population of a province "*includes, where the number of children so warrants, the right to have them receive that instruction in <u>minority language educational facilities</u> provided out of public funds*". In the French version of this section, the chain of qualifiers was translated as "*des établissements d'enseignement de la minorité linguistique*" (lit.: "*language educational facilities of the minority*"). In a reference on minority language education rights[212], the Ontario

Court of Appeal held that the phrase could mean either *"educational facilities for the minority language"* or *"language educational facilities of the minority"*. Since the French version of the Charter expressed only this second meaning[213], the Court held that the section's meaning was that which was common to both versions.

Some words which have extended meanings can also be difficult to translate. The two meanings might be translated with two different words, which might be confusing for someone comparing the two texts. The word claim for example can have a different

---

[212] *Re Education Act of Ontario and Minority Language Education Rights*, (1984) 47 OR (2nd) 1 (CA).

[213] In French, the first meaning of the phrase would have been translated as *"des établissements déstinés à l'enseignement de la langue de la minorité"*.

meaning when used as a plural: *the claims* often means *the amount of claims*.

Two examples show how this same word can be used in two very different ways:

1) *Before paying out a share of money payable to an owner, the trustee shall deduct from the money <u>the claims</u> against the owner that secure the payment of money.*

    Avant de verser à un propriétaire la part des sommes qui lui sont payables, le fiduciaire prélève sur celle-ci <u>le montant des réclamations</u> présentées au propriétaire qui garantissent le paiement des sommes. (the underlined segment literally means *the amount of claims*).

2) <u>*A claim*</u> *shall not be made after the second anniversary of the date on which <u>the claim</u> was discovered.*

> Aucune réclamation ne peut être présentée après le deuxième anniversaire du jour où sont découverts les faits qui ont donné naissance à la réclamation. (the underlined words literally mean *"the facts that give rise to the claim"*)[214].

The ambiguities contained by legal terms of common use such as *claim* show how easily translation mistakes can occur if the translators are not trained in law.

When a word or a concept exists in one language and not in the other, it will normally be expressed by a periphrasis in the second language. This periphrasis might present only

---

[214] Examples cited by Michael J.B. Wood, p. 73 in *Drafting Bilingual Legislation in Canada: Examples of Beneficial Cross-Pollination Between the Two Language Versions*, Statute Law Review, Volume 17, Number 1, pp. 66-77, 1996.

one aspect of the concept, leaving out other aspects that would have been implied in the first language. When translating a somewhat vague concept, the periphrasis can also turn out to be much more precise in its expression. Such preciseness would thus change the intended meaning of the sentence.

Similarly, adjectival modifiers are usually expressed in greater detail in French than in English. The following example illustrates the problem that such a discrepancy may pose:

The centre <u>nearest to</u> the person shall conduct the evaluation.

Le centre <u>le plus proche de l'endroit où se trouve</u> la personne procède à l'évaluation. (*the centre nearest to where the person finds her/himself shall conduct the evaluation*)[215].

---

[215] Example cited by Michael J.B. Wood, p. 73 in *Drafting Bilingual Legislation in Canada: Examples of Beneficial Cross-Pollination Between the Two Language Versions*, Statute Law Review, Volume 17, Number 1, pp. 66-

In French, the translation of *nearest* requires precisions that were not given in the English version of the sentence. Which centre should have the jurisdiction? The one nearest to what? The place where the person lives, works, happens to be at a precise moment?

In order to avoid such problems, drafters and translators strive to be precise in their phrasing and anticipate all forms of ambiguity. The English language and the French language are not by nature incompatible, but ensuring this compatibility requires extra work and attention to detail. Although the "natural" way to phrase the aforementioned sentence is ambiguous, an unambiguous phrasing could easily be found which could still be idiomatic and easy to understand, for instance: *The centre nearest to the residence of the person shall conduct the evaluation.*

77, 1996.

The examples given above dealt with English-to-French ambiguities but similar problems can occur the other way round, when using French as the first working language.

Many of these idiomatic ambiguities (and their consequences) can be avoided by steering clear from certain terms and resorting to more specific ones. This question has progressively been taken into account by drafters and translators.

(2) Adopting a simple style

Lexical considerations left aside, style also can have a considerable influence on the expression of the same idea in two languages.

Canadian English-language laws are the heirs of Westminster's traditions and style.

For most of its existence the country was ruled by laws passed by the British Parliament or laws made in Canada with the same vocabulary and style. The French legacy also had an influence in French-speaking Canada but this influence met that of Westminster. The end result is a mixed French Canadian legal language which differs from the French legal language and has developed affinities with the English style.

Stylistic techniques have been developed by drafters and translators over the course of the years to avoid ambiguities or difficulties in the expression.

The use of short sentences can also make the understanding (and translation) of a law easier. Readers need to pause to assimilate a message and long sentences might not allow this. Writers in French tend to avoid long sentences more than writers in English do[216]. Sections or subsections that consist in one long English sentence often consist of several short sentences in French[217].

The use of the active voice rather than the passive voice can also help avoid diverging meanings. When using the active voice, the drafter is forced to specify an actor for the sentence. If a text creates an obligation but does not specify clearly on whom it is imposed, it would be hard to rely on it in case

---

[216] See p. 74, Michael J.B. Wood, *Drafting Bilingual Legislation in Canada: Examples of Beneficial Cross-Pollination Between the Two Language Versions*, Statute Law Review, Volume 17, Number 1, pp. 66-77, 1996.

[217] In Ontario for instance, subsection 23(3) of the *Ontario Legislative Drafting Conventions* acknowledges the fact that the language structure of French makes this result inevitable. –See p. 74, Michael J.B. Wood, *Drafting Bilingual Legislation in Canada: Examples of Beneficial Cross-Pollination Between the Two Language Versions*, Statute Law Review, Volume 17, Number 1, pp. 66-77, 1996.

the obligation is not fulfilled[218]. On this point too, English and French differ. French tends to resort more often to the active voice than English. In English it is normal usage to use the passive voice when no actor needs to be specified. In such cases in French, the active voice would still prevail with an impersonal construction.

English is spoken here would be said *On parle anglais ici* (*One speaks English here*).

Contemporary English-language legislation is different from that which was made 100 years ago in that the concern for translatability has been incorporated to the

---

[218] As was the case for instance in *R. v. Elm Tree nursing home Inc.* (1987) 20 OAC 277 – See p. 74, Michael J.B. Wood, *Drafting Bilingual Legislation in Canada: Examples of Beneficial Cross-Pollination Between the Two Language Versions*, Statute Law Review, Volume 17, Number 1, pp. 66-77, 1996.

drafting stage. Translators find it much harder to translate laws of the early 20th century than laws from the end of this same century: habits of expression have changed[219].

---

[219] The example of Ontario illustrates this change. Since 1978 all of the province's main laws have been translated into French. *"Current Ontario statutes were drafted over the past 100 years. In that time, the English drafting method and style has gone through continuous change. The most recent statutes are found by translators to be easier to translate into comfortable French than the older ones. Developments in English drafting can be speeded up. Many characteristics of the English statutes are in control of the draftsman. They exist only as habits, not essential to the law, and continue because, in English, they cause no problem. The characteristics of English drafting, often pointed to as a cultural difference, are not seen in that way by the English draftsman. He sees two principal governing factors: the expectation of the judicial system and his own drafting ability. His principal objective is clear communication. It is, therefore, entirely possible to change habits of expression only"*, See p. 124, Arthur N. Stonet, *Bilingual drafting in a Common law jurisdiction in Canada*, Statute Law Review, 1987.

c) The material constraints

Two main constraints weigh on the production of bilingual laws and statutes: time and money.

No matter what option is chosen to prepare bilingual legislation, it usually takes more time than preparing unilingual legislation.

In the case of the method of subsequent translation, a lot of pressure is usually put on the translators. While the drafters are considered to be doing the most important part of the work, the translators' work is often seen as a mere formality, they are therefore expected to work much faster. This time constraint can prevent them from having the opportunity to get well acquainted with the subject-matter of the law and ask all the questions they want to the drafter.

The drafters themselves are often under pressure to produce bills fast. Bilingual drafting thus means that either less time is spent on each draft or that less drafts are produced. The only way to keep up with the needs of the institutions is therefore to hire more staff, which brings up the other material constraint, namely money.

Bilingualism has a cost and this cost is not always easy to bear.

A unilingual province like Ontario has translated its most important pieces of legislation into French and produces bilingual legislation since 1978. Ontario's total authoring and publishing budget is US$ 2,65 million (which includes the salaries of a fourteen-member English drafting team and a fourteen-member translation team). In contrast, Nunavut whose laws are for the moment mainly in English and French cannot afford to have them translated in its main language (Inuktitut). Ontario's authoring and publishing budget is the equivalent of that of the whole Nunavut Legal Services Board[220].

[220] See p. 20, D.G. Patterson, *Nunavut Legal Services Study: Final Report*, Department of Justice Canada (Ottawa, 2004).

[221] For Donald L. Revell, the obstacle constituted by costs might endanger Nunavut's legal system. "*In a jurisdiction such as Nunavut, where the laws are in English and French but not in the native language (...), the failure to find the money to translate may have significant implications elsewhere in the system. The failure to pass laws in Inuktitut is seen as a failure to realize these ambitions. If credible translation work does not begin soon, the whole legal system will lose credibility. But Nunavut, with a population of 25,000, may, in my opinion, find that the cultural and political imperative cannot overcome the cost issue*". – See p. 1102, Donald L. Revell, *Authoring bilingual laws: the importance of process*, Brook. J. Int'l. L. Vol. 29:3 2004, pp. 1085-1105

Costs can therefore constitute a real obstacle to the achievement of legal bilingualism[221].

2. The Federal legislature

The federal Parliament established by the *B.N.A. Act* was modelled after the British Parliament[222]. The lower house, the House of Commons, is composed of elected members like its British counterpart. The Prime Minister and the Cabinet are formed within the majority party at the House of Commons.

The Senate is the Canadian upper house. As is the case in the British House of Lords its members are not elected[223] they are nominated by the Governor in Council (following the recommendations of the Prime

---

[222] Canada was still under British authority until the Canadian Constitution was repatriated in 1982.

[223] Members of the British House of Lords are either hereditary peers or life peers (appointed by the crown). In Canada

Minister). Senators are nominated to serve until they reach the age of 75.

The *B.N.A. Act* granted the federal Parliament the power to pass laws for the *"peace, order and good government of Canada"*[224]. It also gave Parliament exclusive power over taxation, national defence, citizenship, banking, criminal law[225], Indians (and Indian lands), trade and fisheries. Power was to be shared in other areas such as immigration, agriculture and social policy. Finally, the Act also listed sixteen specific areas of provincial responsibility, including education and municipal institutions.

[224] Cf. *British North America Act*, 1867, Section 91.

[225] A single Criminal Code is applied throughout Canada. The particularity is that in criminal matters the courts of first instance are the provincial courts (the administration of justice relies on provincial courts and on municipal police forces). The provinces do not legislate on criminal matters, but they can promulgate quasi-criminal offences in a variety of areas (administrative and others).

Everything in the federal Parliament, from the way statutes were written to the way debates were organised, resembled the practices of Westminster.

As mentioned earlier, since the beginning of the British rule in Canada, French-language and English-language laws have coexisted. One century later, section 133 of the *B.N.A. Act* recognised both English and French as the country's official languages and provided for the publication of federal statutes in both languages.

Yet this obligation did not result in an effectively bilingual federal Parliament. Most parliamentary debates did indeed take place in English. This unilingualism was reinforced by both the majority of Parliamentarians being Anglophones[226] and by the fact that the

British laws constituted the core of the Canadian legal order[227].

Simultaneous translation of debates in the federal parliament only began in 1954. Before that, representatives of the people who did not speak the language used in debates (usually English) could only have access to bills in the other language at the stage of the second reading[228]. This

---

[226] As mentioned earlier, not only was it more natural for Anglophone parliamentarians to speak English in the Parliament of a British land, there was also a clear reluctance to use French. The minority's rights were recognized but giving more importance to this language would have been a way of keeping alive the culture of this group, which also happened to link it to England's traditional rival and enemy. This was clearly out of the question.

[227] Constitutional acts, such as the *B.N.A. Act* were indeed acts of the British Parliament.

[228] Before the enactment of the *Official Languages Act*, bilingualism in the debates in the House of Commons was governed by rule 74 of the *Standing Rules of the House*

constituted a very concrete impediment to their full participation in the law-making process. It is nonetheless important to mention that French-mother-tongue politicians usually had at least some knowledge of the English language.

Until 1969, the "universal rule" for all federal statutes was that they were drafted in English[229]. The translation into French only

---

of Commons which stated that: "*All bills shall be printed for the second reading in the French and English languages*".

[229] Exceptions were apparently very rare and not related to statutes on major issues (e.g. at the time of the Royal Commission's survey, the single recent exception to the rule involved a statute emanating from the department of Forestry). – See p. 112, Claude-Armand Sheppard, *The Law of Languages in Canada*, Studies of the Royal Commission on Bilingualism and Biculturalism, Information Canada (Ottawa, 1971) ; See also p. 1100, Donald L. Revell, *Authoring bilingual laws: the importance of process*, Brook. J. Int'l. L. Vol. 29:3 2004, pp. 1085-1105.

took place after completion of the final draft in English.

The two versions of the statutes had to be published (pursuant to section 133 of the *B.N.A. Act* – which makes bilingual publishing compulsory but does not specify whether drafting should be bilingual too). Provisions for publication were detailed in several pieces of legislation[230].

The *Official Languages Act* reinforced bilingualism in Parliament. Apart from the obligation to enact, print and publish all acts of Parliament in both languages[231], the Act guaranteed the right to use English and French in the proceedings of Parliament[232], it

---

[230] Namely the *Rules and Orders of the House of Commons*, the *Rules and Orders of the Senate* and the *Act Respecting the Publication of the Statutes*.

[231] Cf. *Official Languages Act*, section 6: "*All Acts of Parliament shall be enacted, printed and published in both official languages*".

also provided for bilingual reports[233], records and journals[234].

Following the movement of pro-active official bilingualism in the 1960s and 1970s, the drafting method for federal laws changed. From 1978 onwards, co-drafting replaced unilingual drafting followed by translation[235].

---

[232] Cf. *Official Languages Act*, subsection 4(1): *"English and French are the official languages of Parliament, and everyone has the right to use either of those languages in any debates and other proceedings of Parliament"*.

[233] Cf. *Official Languages Act*, subsection 4(3): *"Everything reported in official reports of debates or other proceedings of Parliament shall be reported in the official langua ge in which it was said and a translation thereof into the other official language shall be included therewith"*.

[234] Cf. *Official Languages Act*, subsection 5: *"The journals and other records of Parliament shall be made and kept, and shall be printed and published, in both official languages"*.

[235] The adoption of co-drafting on the federal scale took some time. In 1966 already, Minister of Justice Lucien Cardin announced at the House of Commons that steps were taken to provide for simultaneous drafting rather than

The French versions of all major federal laws were also reviewed and revised. As explained earlier, this change of method was aimed at guaranteeing the equal authority of the two versions of each federal statute[236]. All federal Canadian statutes are now produced through co-drafting.

translation: "*I (...) propose for the sake of accuracy and clarity to take whatever steps are necessary to draft legislation in each of the two languages in order to avoid the difficulty of interpreting translated law*". – See p. 115, Claude-Armand Sheppard, *The Law of Languages in Canada*, Studies of the Royal Commission on Bilingualism and Biculturalism, Information Canada (Ottawa, 1971).

[236] "*Ottawa, by the late 1960s had generated the political will to accommodate the emergence of a strong French culture and, by 1978, moved to co-drafting. According to federal officials with whom I have spoken, co-drafting was part of the federal effort to give the highest possible credibility to the French versions of its laws, additionally all existing French versions were reviewed and revised to assure their legal and linguistic correctness.*", See p. 1100, Donald L. Revell, *Authoring bilingual laws: the importance of process*, Brook. J. Int'l. L. Vol. 29:3 2004.

3. Provincial legislatures

New Brunswick is the only officially bilingual province in Canada. There, like on the federal level, the method used to prepare legislation is co-drafting.

Although the other provinces are not officially bilingual, they all have some bilingual laws. In these provinces the authoring of legislation is divided in two stages: drafting and translating.

The first step in the authoring process is the same in most provinces. The clients (various government departments) supply the office of legislative counsel with policy instructions. An authoring team composed of one or more drafters, one or more translators and one or more linguistic revisors is assigned to the project (depending on the nature of the project the size of the team will vary). The drafter will review the client's instructions, ask for clarifications or details, do legal research and finally write the document. When the drafter is satisfied of the draft and the client does not require any amendments, the draft is transmitted to the translator[237].

The second step is the translation. The translator's job is to prepare a text which accurately reflects the original while being linguistically correct. This stage usually involves consultations between the drafter and the translator. Once completed, the translation is reviewed by a linguistic revisor (a senior translator). The text of both versions is sometimes reviewed by a bilingual revisor

---

[237] See p. 34, Donald L. Revell, *Bilingual Legislation: The Ontario Experience*, Statute Law Review, Volume 19, Number 1, pp. 32-40, 1998.

who ensures that the two versions have the same legal meaning. In some provinces (e.g. Ontario), these revisors are lawyers.

4. Subordinate legislation

Subordinate legislation is an often overlooked part of legislation, yet it plays a relatively important role in the administration of public affairs. Subordinate legislation gained importance during the 19th and 20th centuries as the power of central and local government authorities grew.

Subordinate legislation comes in many forms: regulations, rules, orders, by-laws, ordinances and orders-in-council. It exists at federal, provincial, territorial and municipal levels. This field of legislation, because of its breadth, is not easy to survey.

The scope of this dissertation does not allow for its in-depth examination. Only a general overview will be made.

One should first note that a large share of federal subordinate legislation has been subject to the obligation of bilingualism long before the *Official Languages Act*. Orders of general application were (and are) usually in the jurisdiction of the *Regulations Act*. An English and a French version of these regulations had (and still have) to be published. The production of these two versions was similar to that of bilingual statutes: a first version was drafted (usually in English) and translated. Drafting was made by the department or agency concerned. Translations were either made by the department produced the first version or by translators seconded from the Federal Translation Bureau[238].

Like for most of Canada's federal legislation, the *Official Languages Act* constituted a turning point for regulations. The act provides that federal subordinate legislation has to be made in both languages[239]

---

[238] See p. 119-134, Claude-Armand Sheppard, *The Law of Languages in Canada*, Studies of the Royal Commission on Bilingualism and Biculturalism, Information Canada (Ottawa, 1971)

[239] Cf. *Official Languages Act*, section 7: *"(1) Any instrument made in the execution of a legislative power conferred by or under an Act of Parliament that*

> *(a) is made by, or with the approval of, the Governor in Council or one or more ministers of the Crown,*
>
> *(b) is required by or pursuant to an Act of Parliament to be published in the Canada Gazette, or*
>
> *(c) is of a public and general nature*

shall be made in both official languages and, if printed and published, shall be printed and published in both official languages.

. If it is to be printed and published, this has to be done in both languages too.

Concerning provincial, territorial and municipal subordinate legislation, the situation varies from one part of the country to the other. The rule of thumb is that where there is a significant French-speaking or

---

(2) All instruments made in the exercise of a prerogative or other executive power that are of a public and general nature shall be made in both official languages and, if printed and published, shall be printed and published in both official languages.
(3) Subsection (1) does not apply to
(a) an ordinance of the Northwest Territories or a law made by the legislature of Yukon, or the legislature of Nunavut, or any instrument made under any such ordinance or law, or
(b) a by-law, law or other instrument of an Indian band, band council or other body established to perform a governmental function in relation to an Indian band or other group of aboriginal people,
by reason only that the ordinance, by-law, law or other instrument is of a public and general nature."

English-speaking minority subordinate legislation is bilingual. This was advised by the Royal Commission on Bilingualism and Biculturalism and followed in most provinces[240].

---

[240] See *History of Canadian Language Politics*, Mapleleafweb.com (Department of Political Science, University of Lethbridge, Canada).

VI. THE CANADIAN JUDICIARY AND LANGUAGE

The Canadian court system is composed of provincial, territorial, federal and special courts. Each province has inferior and intermediate courts as well as a superior court (sometimes called Supreme Court).

On the federal scale, there are various boards and commissions topped by the Federal Court (formerly Exchequer Court). This court deals with matters outside the jurisdiction of any single province, as well as some specific areas of federal law (e.g. taxation, customs, administrative law...). It has exclusive jurisdiction in some areas (e.g. patent) or shares jurisdiction is some others (e.g. admiralty).

There are also several special judicial bodies with a pan-Canadian jurisdiction such as the tax review board or the Canadian transport commission.

The apex of the Canadian court system is the Supreme Court whose duties are to hear appeals from these courts and deliver references. The provincial and federal systems are integrated in that cases may be appealed from provincial level to the Supreme Court of Canada[241].

By law, all federal courts are bilingual[242]. Provincial courts are not necessarily bilingual but must provide interprets to parties who do

---

[241] See p. 55-56, Alan N. Katz, *Legal traditions and systems*, Greenwood Press (Westport, United States of America, 1986)

[242] Cf. Section 133 of the *B.N.A. Act*, Section 19 of the *Canadian Charter of Rights and Freedoms*

not understand the language of the proceedings[243].

In the Canadian legal order where judgments become precedents and shape the law, clear expression is as important in a court decision as it is in a statute. The same difficulties evoked earlier concerning the making of bilingual laws are encountered by court personnel in order to fulfil the objectives of bilingual justice. Their task could be considered to be even more arduous, if one bears in mind that they do not only get to interpret statutes or previous cases (and their potential differences in English and French), they also need to conduct proceedings in one or two languages as well as draft unambiguous decisions.

---

[243] Cf. section 14 of the *Canadian Charter of Rights and Freedoms*.

The preparation and issuance of bilingual judgments present the same challenges as the production of bilingual legislation. These aspects having been presented in the previous part, they will not be detailed here. It is nonetheless important to bear in mind that such considerations (translation, bilingual drafting, linguistic ambiguities, style and material constraints) play an non negligible part in the making of bilingual judgments.

1. Courts of first instance

a) Provincial courts

Each province and territory has its own courts. While most provinces are unlingual, several have bilingual courts or translation services.

Moreover, pursuant to the *Canadian Charter of Rights and Freedoms*, interpreters are to be provided when parties to a trial do not understand the language of the proceedings.

In Canada criminal legislation is passed by the federal Parliament[244]. Yet it is provincial not federal courts that hear criminal cases in first instance. They all rely on the same *Criminal Code* throughout the country. The Code has been amended in 1988 to allow the use of either official language in criminal cases. There is therefore a form of official bilingualism in criminal matters in provincial courts.

---

[244] Provinces can only enact subordinate legislation concerning quasi-criminal offences.

The scope of this dissertation does not allow a lengthy and detailed presentation of linguistic practices in each province's courts. Such a presentation would also be fastidious, as the main division to be found in this field is between English-speaking provinces and Quebec. In the former, unilingualism is the rule, bilingualism the exception. Even so, the right to an interpreter (1) has prevented this unilingualism from denying French-speakers (or Allophones[245]) fair access to justice.

In Quebec (2), where Canada's tradition of bilingualism was founded there have been attempts to enforce a French unilingualism in the past decades. The result is a French-dominated bilingualism.

---

[245] In the Canadian context, the term Allophone refers to someone who is neither an Anglophone nor a Francophone.

It seems in fact that pure bilingualism at the provincial scale only exists in New Brunswick (3), Canada's only officially bilingual province.

Another element in the Canadian institutional landscape is the newly created province of Nunavut (4), which counts no less than eight official languages.

(1) The right to an interpreter

The only general rule concerning language in provincial courts (and as a matter of fact in all courts) is the aforementioned right to an interpreter granted by section 14 of the *Canadian Charter of Rights and Freedoms*. Before 1982, this right was also protected by the 1960 *Canadian Bill of Rights*[246].

This language right is fundamental in that it guarantees, regardless of one's language, that parties and witnesses to judicial proceedings understand and are understood.

This right is not one which must necessarily have been invoked or asserted in order to be enjoyed. The recourse to the right to an interpreter cannot be denied on the grounds that the person is able to speak some English/French. If a party/witness to proceedings asserts that s/he does not

---

[246] In section 2(g): no law of Canada shall be construed or applied so as to *"deprive a person of the right to the assistance of an interpreter in any proceedings in which he is involved or in which he is a party or a witness, before a court, commission, board or other tribunal, if he does not understand or speak the language in which the proceedings are conducted"*.

understand the language or that s/he is deaf, the request for an interpreter ought to be granted unless compelling evidence is adduced which enables the judge to conclude that this request was not made in good faith[247]. Nothing in section 14 requires judges to conduct an enquiry into the ability or disability of the person who asks for an interpreter. Nor does section 14 impose a duty on the court to inform parties to a trial of their right to an interpreter. But if it is apparent that such assistance is needed, it ought to be provided by the court, even in cases when no request was made[248]. If a person then clearly chooses

---

[247] The opposing party has the right to challenge a request for the assistance of an interpreter. The party who raised the objection can call witnesses to testify as to the linguistic competence of the subject. To come to a decision, the judge or chairman of the tribunal will have to consider both the good faith of the person who requested an interpreter and her/his legitimate desire to express her/himself in the language s/he knows best.

not to exercise her/his right, s/he cannot subsequently claim that her/his right was infringed. It is also important to note that section 14 gives a right to the parties to a proceeding but not to their lawyers[249].

In the context of often non-bilingual provincial courts, the right granted by section 14 seems to be the next best thing.

(2) The case of Quebec

Quebec is the only province whose sole official language is French. It is also (as explained earlier) the province where official bilingualism started[250].

---

[248] Cf. *R. v. Tsang* (1985), 27 C.C.C. (3d) 365 (B.C.C.A.)

[249] Cf. *Cormier v. Fournier* (1986), 29 D.L.R. (4th) 675 (N.B.Q.B.)

[250] See II, C, 3), c) (3)

Since the British took over French Canada, virtually all of Quebec's institutions have been bilingual. This official bilingualism, enshrined in section 133 of the 1867 *B.N.A. Act*[251] was not seriously challenged until the enactment of the *Charter of the French Language*[252] in 1977. Up to that point, Quebec was the only part of Canada with well-established bilingual institutions[253].

Among other things, in its section 13, the *Charter of the French Language* stated that all court decisions had to be issued in French or have a French version. In cases where two language versions existed, only the

[251] See above II, A, 1: A first step towards official bilingualism: the British North America Act

[252] See above II, A, 7: Resistance in Quebec: The Charter of the French Language

[253] See p. 161, Claude-Armand Sheppard, *The Law of Languages in Canada*, Studies of the Royal Commission on Bilingualism and Biculturalism, Information Canada (Ottawa, 1971).

French one would be recognised as official[254]. This provision which was only one aspect of Quebec's new unilingualism (introduced by the Charter) was held *ultra vires* the Constitution[255] by the Supreme Court. Section

---

[254] And the Charter itself was only published in French at first. Section 13: *"Les jugements rendus au Québec par les tribunaux et les organismes exerçant des fonctions judiciaires ou quasi-judiciaires doivent être rédigés en français ou être accompagnés d'une version française dûment authentifiée. Seule la version française du jugement est officielle. "* (Judgments delivered in Québec by courts, judicial and quasi-judicial bodies must be written in French or be accompanied by a duly authenticated French version. Only the French version of a judgment is official).

[255] Section 13 of the *Charter of the French Language* constituted a violation of section 133 of the *B.N.A. Act*: *"not only is the option to use either language given to any person involved in proceedings before the Courts of Québec or its other adjudicative tribunals... but documents emanating from such bodies or issued in their name or under their authority may be in either language, and this option extends to the issuing and publication of judgments or other orders."* in *Attorney General of Québec v. Blaikie,* (case also known as

13 has since been withdrawn, but Quebec has remained officially unilingual. Even though English can be used in the provincial parliament and in court, most of the legislation and the case-law are drafted in French, which makes it the language of reference. The Supreme Court of Canada also tends (and tended) to issue its decisions regarding Quebec in French[256]. All of this results in a French predominance in the law of Quebec.

"*Blaikie n°1*"), (1979) 2 S.C.R. 1016 at 1030.

[256] Before 1969, the Supreme Court of Canada tended to issue its judgments or references concerning Quebec in French. Since 1969 (and the first Official Languages Act), the Supreme Court issues its judgments in both English and French, but in matters concerning Quebec, the original version of the judgment is usually in French (therefore, in case of difference between the two versions, more importance might be given to the French version in the interpretation). – See below III, D., 2, b), (1) Language(s) of work.

(3) The case of New Brunswick

New Brunswick is the only officially bilingual province in Canada. Its bilingualism is enshrined in the Canadian Constitution, namely in the *Canadian Charter of Rights and Freedoms*[257]. The Charter also guarantees bilingualism in New Brunswick courts in its section 19(2)[258].

---

[257] Section 16(2) of the *Canadian Charter of Rights and Freedoms* provides that: "*English and French are the official languages of New Brunswick and have equality of status and equal rights and privileges as to their use in all institutions of the legislature and government of New Brunswick*".

[258] Section 19(2) of the Canadian Charter of Rights and Freedoms provides that: "*Either English or French may be used by any person in, or in any pleading in, or in process issuing from, any court of New Brunswick*".

The sections of the Charter dealing with languages in New Brunswick are identical in their phrasing as the ones regarding the federal state. In consequence, the province's courts function exactly like federal courts (as far as languages are concerned).

New Brunswick's *Official Languages Act*[259] contains details regarding these language rights in the administration of justice. Section 17 provides that *"Every person has the right to use the official language of his or her choice in any matter before the courts, including all proceedings, or in any pleading or process issuing from a court"*. Section 18 secures this right by stating that *"No person shall be placed at a disadvantage by reason of the choice made under section 17"*. An obligation

---

[259] The first *Official Languages Act* of New Brunswick was adopted in 1969. The version of June 2002 is cited here. – This act reiterates the provisions of the federal *Official Languages Act* on the provincial scale.

is placed on the court to understand the language(s) chosen by the parties to proceedings (Section 19)[260]. The accused have the right to be heard in the language of their choice (Section 20). Witnesses too have the right to express themselves in the language of their choice (Section 21)[261]. Whenever Her Majesty (in right of the province or an institution) is party to civil proceedings the language used by Her Majesty will be that chosen by the other party (Section 22)[262].

---

[260] The Court must understand the language(s) chose by the parties without the help of an interpreter or any process of simultaneous translation or consecutive interpretation.

[261] Upon the request of one of the parties or the witness, the court has the duty to ensure that services of simultaneous translation or consecutive interpretation are available to the person who made the request.

[262] In cases where parties to civil proceedings (other than Her Majesty or a public institution) fail to agree on the official language to be used in the proceedings, Her Majesty

Decisions, orders or judgments are to be published in both languages where they determine a question of law of importance and when the proceedings were conducted in whole or in part in both official languages (Section 24).

All these elements draw a clear parallel between the New Brunswick courts and the federal courts. This system is often presented as ideal in terms of language rights. Parties to a trial can indeed express themselves in their own language and be understood directly by the court (without the intervention of an interpreter). Trials can take place in two languages and be heard by bilingual judges.

The system is nonetheless costly. Its implementation was also made possible by

---

or the institution concerned will use such official language as is reasonable depending on the circumstances (Section 23) the presence of a substantial French-speaking population in New Brunswick (one third of the total population). New Brunswick has the largest proportion of Francophones outside of Quebec. In other provinces the very legitimacy and feasibility (in terms of human resources) of such a bilingual system would have been questioned.

(4) The case of Nunavut

The region now known as Nunavut[263] has supported a continuous population for approximately 4000 years. Negotiations for a land claim agreement between the Inuit and the federal government started in 1976. A land claims agreement was decided in September 1992 and approved by nearly 85% of the voters of what was to become the province of Nunavut. The *Nunavut Act* which created the province was passed in 1993 and the transition was completed in 1999.

While it is the least populated province in Canada (28,700 inhabitants in 2002[264]), it is the one with the greatest number of official languages. Its eight official languages are

---

[263] Nunavut means "*our land*" in Inuktitut.

[264] Source: Microsoft Encarta Reference Library 2004.

Chipewyan, Cree, Dogrib, English, French, Gwich'in, Inuktitut and Slavey[265]. The government's working language is Inuktitut[266].

Prior to the creation of the province, the current territory of Nunavut was part of the Northwest Territories and as such under the jurisdiction of the Territorial Court and the Northwest Territories' Supreme Court. Since 1999, all types of cases are heard by Nunavut's one and only court, the Nunavut Court of Justice[267]. The legal authority of the Court is both provincial and federal[268].

---

[265] Cf. *Official Languages Act* of the Northwest Territories, section 2.

[266] It is also the mother-tongue of 49% of Nunavut's inhabitants - See p. 13, D.G. Patterson, *Nunavut Legal Services Study: Final Report*, Department of Justice Canada (Ottawa, 2004).

[267] Although the Nunavut justice system was originally meant to have two levels (with a Nunavut Supreme Court), in the end a single court (with the status of Superior Court) was set up. This choice was made to simplify

One singularity of the Nunavut Court of Justice is that it is also a circuit court. One branch of the court remains in Iqaluit (the Court's headquarters) and one branch travels around the province. This second branch travels to approximately 85% of the communities across the province[269]. The court travels to the communities every six weeks to

---

the legal system. – See p. 18, D.G. Patterson, *Nunavut Legal Services Study: Final Report*, Department of Justice Canada (Ottawa, 2004).

[268] The Court is backed by Justices of the Peace who are intended to hear a wider range of cases than is common in the rest of Canada. This is meant to relieve the Court of its big amount of cases but the Justices of the Peace have not managed to achieve this for the moment. See p. ix, D.G. Patterson, *Nunavut Legal Services Study: Final Report*, Department of Justice Canada (Ottawa, 2004).

[269] The court only travels to the bigger communities. The smaller communities are not visited by the court. – See the website of the Nunavut Court of Justice (http://www.nucj.ca/unifiedcourt.htm)

two years depending on the number of charges coming from these communities.

The Court has an average of two to three court sittings per week (at least one of the circuit court and one in Iqaluit).

Members of the circuit court include a judge, a clerk, a court reporter, a prosecutor and at least one defence attorney. Depending on the cases to be heard other court workers and victim/witness assistants may travel along.

Various languages are spoken in the communities visited by the circuit court and interpreters are very often resorted to. The usual practice is to hire interpreters in the communities but in some cases interpreters can be hired from other communities and brought to the court sitting.

Court sittings take place in community halls, school gyms and other facilities depending on availability. All the proceedings are interpreted for the public. Elders and justices of the peace sit with the judge in the courtroom and are given the opportunity to speak with the accused following sentencing submissions and prior to the passing of the sentence.

This community-based approach to justice is quite different from that of the other provinces, even though similar systems have been set up in Aboriginal communities throughout Canada[270]. Nunavut's singularity lies in the fact that Aboriginal (in this case Inuit) ways govern most aspects of functioning of the judiciary, not just some.

---

[270] As explained before, Aboriginal communities throughout Canada have progressively regained the right to manage the justice in their communities. Resort to methods such as the sentencing circles is now common and well accepted by mainstream Canadian courts.

The Department of Justice of Nunavut fully endorses this approach. On its website, an introductory statement explains that: *"The Department promotes and protects a peaceful society through the administration of a justice system which respects the role of community members in maintaining harmony, and which adheres to the principles and values of Inuit Qaujimajatuqangit[271]"*[272].

The recourse to interpreters seems to be the most efficient way to deal with all of Nunavut's official languages. The fact that

---

[271] The *Inuit Qaujimajatuqangit* is an Inuktitut expression often translated as Inuit traditional knowledge, Inuit traditional institutions or Inuit traditional technology. In the context of this quote, the closest translation could be to be the Inuit legacy and traditions or the Inuit culture and traditions. It is interesting to note that the expression has not been translated into English (or in French).

[272] Excerpt from the official presentation of the Department of Justice of Nunavut. – See http://www.justice.gov.nu.ca

these interpreters are often the peers of the parties to the proceedings is another indicator of the communal character of justice in the province. The presence of an interpreter for the public also differs from mainstream Canadian practices (which do not grant a right of information to linguistic minorities of non-official languages). In Nunavut, trials are interpreted for the public because most often they are not considered to concern only the parties, they are perceived as concerning the whole community; hence the presence of the elders (and their right to participate). In other parts of Canada, if mayors or city counsellors were invited to sit in court next to the judge, people would denounce it as a breach of the separation in powers, as a violation of the independence of the judiciary. Things are different in Nunavut where the justice system remained in tune with the ancient traditions and ways.

As a provincial court, the Nunavut Court of Justice can hear cases in Nunavut's eight official languages. As a federal court, it is supposed to use English and/or French. The fact that most of the province's inhabitants are not native English or French speakers does not make things simpler.

During the Court's short existence, language does not seem to have been perceived as a problematic issue. Yet in time, cases might arise where Inuktitut mother-tongue lawyers of Inuktitut mother-tongue parties plead in English before Inuktitut mother-tongue justices. With the development of the province and the influence of mainstream Canadian culture, the communal vision of justice might be rejected by some citizens. Cases where Canadian fundamental rights conflict with *Inuit Qaujimajatuqangit* might arise as well.

Only time will tell in what directions Nunavut's justice system will evolve. It is for the moment a unique system which has found ways to handle linguistic and legal diversity[273].

b) Federal courts

The *B.N.A. Act* of 1867 marked the birth of Canada as a confederation. It was to have a federal parliament and a general court of appeal. The *B.N.A. Act* recognised English and French as the official languages to be used in courts of Canada established under this Act.

---

[273] As mentioned earlier, Aboriginal traditions vary from community to community. To that – in the case of Nunavut – one has to add the law inherited from the Northwest Territories and federal law.

Several federal judicial or quasi-judicial bodies were created under the Act, the main ones being the Supreme Court (see below III, D, 2), the Federal Court (formerly known as the Exchequer Court) and the military courts[274].

The *Exchequer Court Act* which created the Exchequer Court contained no provisions about French-speaking judges or judges from Quebec and until 1969 opinions were only occasionally written in French.

The courts martial and military courts established by the *National Defence Act* apparently[275] also fell under section 133 of the

---

[274] See p. 159, Claude-Armand Sheppard, *The Law of Languages in Canada*, Studies of the Royal Commission on Bilingualism and Biculturalism, Information Canada (Ottawa, 1971).

[275] According to Claude-Armand Sheppard, these courts were governed by section 133 of the *B.N.A. Act*. Indeed they were created after the *B.N.A. Act*, as part of the national defence structure. The link with the mandate given

B.N.A. Act. Bilingualism was not very developed in the Canadian armed forces (some would even have said that it was virtually nonexistent[276]) until the official languages policy of the federal government. It should nonetheless be noted that at that time

---

by the *B.N.A. Act* to the federal authorities is clear. The only way to know if section 133 applied to these courts would have been for someone to be refused the right to use French in military courts and appeal to the Supreme Court. The Supreme Court could have held whether or not section 133 applied to these courts. But Sheppard's study was published after the enactment of the *Official Languages Act*. No such complaint had been made and complaints regarding the linguistic issue in military courts would now rely on the *Official Languages Act*. – See p. 159, Claude-Armand Sheppard, *The Law of Languages in Canada*, Studies of the Royal Commission on Bilingualism and Biculturalism, Information Canada (Ottawa, 1971).

[276] See p. 159, Claude-Armand Sheppard, *The Law of Languages in Canada*, Studies of the Royal Commission on Bilingualism and Biculturalism, Information Canada (Ottawa, 1971).

Canadian military law already provided for interpreters in proceedings.

Until the 1969 *Official Languages Act*, these courts' working language was mainly (and often only) English.

Through its clear requirements, the *Official Languages Act* made bilingualism in federal courts a reality. Unlike the *B.N.A. Act*, it did not state that either language could be used, it provided that both languages had to be used as often as possible in federal courts. These rules were reiterated in the second version of *Official Languages Act* enacted in 1988.

Section 14 of the Act provides that *"English and French are the official languages of the federal courts, and either of those languages may be used by any person in, or in any pleading in or process issuing from, any federal court.".*

Section 16 provides that every federal court has the duty to ensure that every judge or other officer who hears the parties is able to understand the language chosen by the parties without the assistance of an interpreter (if the two languages are used, judges must be bilingual).

Pursuant to section 9, the rules of all federal courts have to be made, printed and published in both official languages.

The first Act provided that all major decisions of federal courts and decisions in bilingual trials had to be issued in both official languages. The second Act provided that in these cases decisions had to be issued simultaneously in both official languages; and that for all other cases decisions issued in one language had to be translated at the earliest possible time[277].

---

[277] *Official Languages Act, 1988, Section 20: (1) Any final decision, order or judgment, including any reasons given therefore, issued by any federal court shall be made available simultaneously in both official languages where*

> *(a) the decision, order or judgment determines a question of law of general public interest or importance; or*
>
> *(b) the proceedings leading to its issuance were conducted in whole or in part in both official languages.*

(2) Where

(a) any final decision, order or judgment issued by a federal court is not required by subsection (1) to be made available simultaneously in both official languages, or

(b) the decision, order or judgment is required by paragraph (1)(a) to be made available simultaneously in both official languages but the court is of the opinion that to make the decision, order or judgment, including any reasons given therefore, available simultaneously in both official languages would occasion a delay prejudicial to the public interest or resulting in injustice or hardship to any party to the proceedings leading to its issuance,

2. The Supreme Court

a) The creation of the Supreme Court

---

the decision, order or judgment, including any reasons given therefore, shall be issued in the first instance in one of the official languages and thereafter, at the earliest possible time, in the other official language, each version to be effective from the time the first version is effective.

(3) Nothing in subsection (1) or (2) shall be construed as prohibiting the oral rendition or delivery, in only one of the official languages, of any decision, order or judgment or any reasons given therefore.

(4) No decision, order or judgment issued by a federal court is invalid by reason only that it was not made or issued in both official languages."

(1) A general court of appeal for Canada

In the constitutional conferences that led to the creation of Canada in 1867, there was very little discussion about creating a Supreme Court.

Section 101 of the 1867 *British North America Act*, the founding constitutional document that joined Canada in a united confederation, authorised Parliament to *"provide for the Constitution, Maintenance, and Organisation of a General Court of Appeal for Canada"*. But this new constitutional order was one of autonomy, not independence. The Privy Council could overrule any decision made by Canadian courts (including that General Court of Appeal).

The creation of a Supreme Court was discussed in the Canadian Parliament several times before an agreement was reached[278]. Some Parliamentarians pointed out the uselessness of such a court as long as the possibility of an appeal to the Privy Council would exist[279].

Other parliamentarians were concerned that a single Supreme Court would not be able to protect the civil law system and its specificities[280].

---

[278] Bills dealing with the creation of a Supreme Court were proposed in 1869 and 1870 but rejected by the Parliamentarians.

[279] Appeals to the Privy Council existed until 1949.

[280] *"Quebec's system of civil law stood, along with religion and language as one of the three pillars of the distinctive culture the preservation of which was a key rationale for granting sovereign powers to provincial legislatures. Although Quebeckers acquiesced in the final power of the Imperial Privy Council to interpret its laws, many of them bitterly resented the prospect of a Court dominated by English Canadians trained in the common law overruling the decisions of Quebec judges on Quebec's Civil Code and Code of Procedure. There were attempts to terminate appeals to*

A compromise was found in 1875 and the *Supreme Court Act* was passed. The compromise was that two out of the six justices would be selected from the bar of Québec[281] and that the Court's jurisdiction in

---

the Supreme Court in provincial law matters or at least to ensure that a majority of judges trained in civil law heard appeals concerning Quebec's distinctive laws. These efforts were not successful. Nor did the Supreme Court issue any self-denying ordinance along the lines of Erie v. Tompkins (U.S. Supreme Court case - 304 U.S. 64 - 1938) *and defer to the decisions of the highest provincial court in provincial law matters. In this respect the Supreme Court's practice reflects the remarkably unitary nature of the Canadian judicial system in which the judges of the provincial courts have jurisdiction in nearly all areas of federal and provincial law"*.
– See p. 6, Peter H. Russell, *Introduction: History and Development of the Court in National Society, The Canadian Supreme Court*, 3 Can. - U.S. L.J. (1980)

[281] The Court was composed of one Chief Justice and five puisne justices all appointed by the Governor in Council (by prerogative the Prime Minister nominated the individuals) among experienced judges or lawyers (a minimum of 10

civil appeals from Québec would only apply to cases involving disputes over a minimum amount of $2,000.

This amount was subsequently raised to $10,000 and finally abolished in 1975. Since then the Court hears civil cases and the only criterion involved in their selection is the importance of the legal issue in dispute.

In 1927, the *Supreme Court Act* was amended to raise the number of justices to seven. In 1949, the Act was amended once more and two positions were added to the bench. One of these two new posts was to be filled by an individual from the Québec bar. In total, three out of nine justices are therefore trained in civil law.

Over the years a custom of regional representation on the bench developed. This

---

years of experience was and still is required).

was aimed at giving provinces a representation that matched their importance. It was also thought that the judges would bring a rich diversity of experience and understanding to the Court[282]. This tacit rule resulted (and still results) in the Court normally being composed of two justices from Western provinces (one of whom is from British Columbia), three justices from Ontario, three from Québec[283] and one from the Atlantic provinces[284]. There is also a

---

[282] See p. 32, Frank Iacobucci, *The Supreme Court of Canada: its history, powers and responsibilities*, 4 J. App. Prac. & Process (2002)

[283] *"It is an iron rule of Canadian politics that Ontario must always have as much if not more than Québec"* – See p. 12, Peter H. Russell, *Introduction: History and Development of the Court in National Society, The Canadian Supreme Court*, 3 Can. – U.S. L.J. (1980)

[284] This custom has existed since the first Supreme Court. At the time, out of six justices, one judge came from the Prairie provinces, one from British Columbia, two from Ontario,

custom that has at least two of the justices from Québec judging every appeal coming from Québec[285].

---

two from Québec and one from the Atlantic provinces.

[285] See p. 158, Claude-Armand Sheppard, *The Law of Languages in Canada*, Studies of the Royal Commission on Bilingualism and Biculturalism, Information Canada (Ottawa, 1971).

(2) The extension of the Court's jurisdiction

aa) A general jurisdiction

Due to Canada's geographic and cultural proximity with the United States, many assume that the Canadian Supreme Court is a replica of the American one. While the two clearly have common features, there are also clear differences between them. One major difference is for instance the type of cases that can be heard. Having been founded as a general court of appeal, the Canadian Supreme Court can hear all types of cases: unlike its counterpart in the United States, its jurisdiction is not limited to federal matters. The case-law of the Supreme Court can therefore have an impact on virtually all fields of law in Canada.

bb) The independence from the Privy Council

During the first decades of its existence as a self-governed autonomous entity, Canada did not really have a Constitution per se. It had the 1867 *B.N.A. Act* (which is now part of the Constitution) which guaranteed Canada's autonomy but subjected its law to the Parliament in Westminster. The Supreme Court's decisions could be overruled by the Privy Council. The possibility of an appeal to the Privy Council minimised the Court's authority and even openly contested it, as the *per saltum* procedure allowed people to appeal directly to the Privy Council without being heard by the Supreme Court.

As early as 1887, the Canadian Parliament tried to suppress this possibility for criminal appeals by amending the *Supreme*

Court Act. Although this amendment remained on books for forty years, the Privy Council struck it down in 1926 as being outside of the powers of the Canadian Parliament. Strengthened by the 1931 *Statute of Westminster* through which the British Parliament granted Canada full political independence, the Canadian Parliament attempted once more to abolish appeals to the Privy Council. Bills to abolish civil and criminal appeals to the Privy Council were presented in the Canadian House of Commons in 1937, 1938 and 1939. The Supreme Court asked to examine the constitutionality of these measures by the Governor in Council held that they were constitutional. An appeal was made to the Privy Council which was unable to answer until the end of World War II. In 1946, the Supreme Court's opinion was affirmed. The Canadian Parliament was allowed to abolish all appeals to the Privy Council. From 1949 onwards, the Supreme Court became Canada's court of last resort[286].

cc) The Court and the Constitution

From 1875 to 1949 most of the cases heard by the Supreme Court concerned private law[287]. Due to the possibility of appealing to the Privy Council, the justices of the Supreme Court were very deferential to the decisions of English courts. In 1949, when the Supreme Court became the court of last

---

[286] See Frank Iacobucci, *The Supreme Court of Canada: its history, powers and responsibilities*, 4 J. App. Prac. & Process (2002)

[287] See p. 5, Peter H. Russell, *Introduction: History and Development of the Court in National Society - The Canadian Supreme Court*, 3 Can. – U.S. L.J. (1980)

resort, public attention focused on its new role as constitutional arbiter.

In 1982, the Canadian Constitution was repatriated and the *Canadian Charter of Rights and Freedoms* came into force. This constitutional enlargement was the beginning of a new era for the Supreme Court. Since the Charter contained extensive provisions on official language rights (sections 16 to 23), the Court became quite active in the protection of these rights[288].

---

[288] See above II, A, 7: Resistance in Québec: the Charter of the French Language

b) Bilingualism at the Supreme Court

(1) Language(s) of work

The Canadian Supreme Court was created pursuant to section 101 of the *B.N.A. Act*. Section 133 of this same Act provides that *"Either the English or the French language (...) may be used by any person or in any pleading or process in or issuing from any court of Canada established under this Act"*. In other words since the creation of the Court, both official languages have always been accepted[289].

In *Macdonald v. The City of Montreal*, the Supreme Court considered the scope of

---

[289] Section 19(1) of the 1982 *Canadian Charter of Rights and Freedoms* contains a similar provision: *"Either English or French may be used by any person in, or in any pleading in or process issuing from, any court established by Parliament"*.

the language rights guaranteed by this section. It held that judges have the right to use the official language of their choice in the writing and issuing of their opinions.

The Court held this section means that all the people who are to submit a statement in court (oral or written) have the right to do it in the language of their choice[290]. They cannot be forced to express themselves in a language which they do not master[291]. In the subsequent case of *Société des Acadiens v.*

---

[290] "*the language rights then protected are those of litigants, counsel, witnesses, judges, and other judicial officers who actually speak, not those of parties or others who are spoken to; and they are those of the writers or issuers of written pleadings and processes, not those of the recipients or readers thereof*" in *Macdonald v. The City of Montreal*, (1986) I S.C.R. 460

[291] Likewise pursuant to section 14 of the *Canadian Charter of Rights and Freedoms* people who do not understand the language in which the proceedings are conducted have the right to an interpreter.

Association of Parents, the Court confirmed that language rights *"vest in the speaker or the writer or issuer of court processes and give the speaker or the writer the constitutionally protected power to speak or to write in the official language of his choice"*[292].

For lawyers involved in appeals before the Supreme Court this choice can be determined by various elements: the mother tongue of the barrister, the mother tongue of the judge to whom a reply or remark might be addressed[293]. The judges then write their opinions in the language of their choice.

---

[292] *Société des Acadiens de Nouveau-Brunswick v. Association of Parents for Fairness in Education* (1986) 1 S.C.R. 549 at 574

[293] See p. 158-159, Claude-Armand Sheppard, *The Law of Languages in Canada*, Studies of the Royal Commission on Bilingualism and Biculturalism, Information Canada (Ottawa, 1971).

aa) 1875 – 1969: An English-speaking Supreme Court

Between 1875 and 1969, the decisions of the Court were reported only in the language of drafting of the individual judges. Although there were sometimes exceptions, normally no translations were provided. The justices from outside of Quebec would draft their opinions in English and the justices from Quebec would use either French or English depending on the case[294]. If the justices from

---

[294] In his 1969 report on the Supreme Court for the Royal Commission on Bilingualism and Biculturalism, Peter Russell noted that: *"The language used when the Court delivers its judgment will depend on the presiding judge and the language used in the litigation. If the presiding judge is French speaking and French was the principal language used in the pleadings, then the judgment will probably be delivered in French. Otherwise it will be in English"* – See p. 92, Peter Russell, *The Supreme Court of Canada as a Bilingual and Bicultural Institution*, Studies of the Royal

Quebec wanted their opinions to be read and taken into account by English-speaking jurists, they were to write them in English[295]. On matters of national interest, decisions would also be written in English. In fact French was only used when a justice chose to use it (usually if it was the language of the parties or the pleadings). English was thus the Court's language by default[296].

Commission on Bilingualism and Biculturalism, Information Canada (Ottawa, 1969)

[295] In the same report Russell remarked that *"This development apparently was prompted by the complaints of English-speaking lawyers against the Court's first few publications of opinions written only in French"* – See p. 93, Peter Russell, *The Supreme Court of Canada as a Bilingual and Bicultural Institution*, Studies of the Royal Commission on Bilingualism and Biculturalism, Information Canada (Ottawa, 1969)

[296] Russell also explained that: *"Since most of the Court's members are English-speaking and these English-speaking judges never write their judgments in French, this means that the bulk of the Court's judgments are reported in*

As mentioned earlier, French was not spoken at the Supreme Court until the appointment of Thibaudeau Rinfret as Chief Justice in 1944. Even then French was used very scarcely. Some efforts towards bilingualism were progressively made. After 1949, by convention, at least two of the three justices from Québec spoke French[297]. In 1964, Supreme Court reports started featuring bilingual headnotes for some important

---

English. The French-speaking judges write opinions in both languages; if the case they are deciding is from Quebec, in all likelihood their opinion will be written in French, whereas if it deals with a matter of national interest, they may express themselves in English" – See p. 93, Peter Russell, *The Supreme Court of Canada as a Bilingual and Bicultural Institution*, Studies of the Royal Commission on Bilingualism and Biculturalism, Information Canada (Ottawa, 1969)

[297] See p. 158, Claude-Armand Sheppard, *The Law of Languages in Canada*, Studies of the Royal Commission on Bilingualism and Biculturalism, Information Canada (Ottawa, 1971).

decisions[298] but this practice was never comprehensive. The Court's seldom use of French soon raised the question of its legitimacy in the eyes of French Canadians[299]. Quebec's Quiet Revolution of the 1960s brought the question of effective bilingualism back on Canada's political agenda.

---

[298] See p. 170, Teresa Scassa, *Language of judgment and the Supreme Court of Canada*, 43 U.N.B.L.J. (1994).

[299] The Court's unilingualism was criticized by Russell in his report to the Royal Commission on Bilingualism and Biculturalism: "*If the Supreme Court is to produce a jurisprudence which can be shared by all Canadians, its decisions must be equally accessible to the country's two major linguistic groups. Up until now this condition has certainly not been fulfilled*" – See p. 95, Peter Russell, *The Supreme Court of Canada as a Bilingual and Bicultural Institution*, Studies of the Royal Commission on Bilingualism and Biculturalism, Information Canada (Ottawa, 1969).

bb) 1970 – 1980: The first *Official Languages Act*

The enactment of the first *Official Languages Act* in 1969 had dramatic consequences on the reporting of Supreme Court decisions. Section 5(1) of the Act provided that all judgments, decisions or orders made by judicial bodies established by an act of the Canadian Parliament had to be issued in both official languages when dealing with *"questions of law of general public interest or importance"* or when the proceedings were conducted (in whole or in part) in both official languages[300].

---

[300] *Official Languages Act* (1969), Section 5(1): *"All final decisions, orders and judgments, including any reasons given therefor, issued by any judicial or quasi-judicial body established by or pursuant to an Act of the Parliament of Canada shall be issued in both official languages where the decision, order or judgment determines a question of law of*

Since the Court's very mandate was to hear and decide *"questions of law of general public interest or importance"*, its decisions were published in both languages from 1970 onwards[301].

The Act did not contain any provisions on the interpretation of judgments published in two languages[302] and during this period, the reports contained no indication of the language in which the decisions had been drafted[303].

---

general public interest or importance or where the proceedings leading to its issue were conducted in whole or in part in both official languages".

[301] They were published side by side in reports. – See p. 171, Teresa Scassa, *Language of judgment and the Supreme Court of Canada*, 43 U.N.B.L.J. (1994).

[302] Nor did the Second *Official Languages Act* (1988) whose article 20 replaced article 5(1) of the first Act.

[303] According to Teresa Scassa, in those days, a good indicator of the language in which a decision had been drafted was the quality of the text. – See p. 171-172, Teresa

This period was that of the tenure of Justice Louis-Philippe Pigeon, an outspoken advocate of bilingualism in the judiciary[304] who personally spent a lot of time proofreading the translations of the judgments to make sure they were accurate[305].

Scassa, *Language of judgment and the Supreme Court of Canada*, 43 U.N.B.L.J. (1994).

[304] See p. 172, Teresa Scassa, *Language of judgment and the Supreme Court of Canada*, 43 U.N.B.L.J. (1994).

[305] According to Chief Justice Brian Dickson, Justice Pigeon's contribution to bilingualism at the Supreme Court was considerable: *"he really played a decisive part in turning the Court into a more bilingual institution than it had ever been before. It goes without saying that justice Pigeon was perfectly bilingual himself. He nonetheless looked deep into the institutional aspects of bilingualism at the Court. He spent a remarkable amount of time and energy to make sure that the translations of the judgments of the Supreme Court of Canada were truthful and accurate"*. – See p. 49-50, Chief Justice Brian Dickson, *Mélanges Louis-Philippe Pigeon*, Wilson & Lafleur (Montreal, 1989).

cc) 1980 – 1988: An English-based bilingualism

In 1980, the Court entered a new period in terms of linguistic practices. The hypothesis of a causality link between this change and Justice Pigeon's death that same year would perhaps be an exaggeration[306]. In any case, the pure bilingualism which he advocated was replaced by another type of bilingualism. The language in which the judgments had been drafted was now mentioned in the reports and the other versions were presented as translations of the judgments. The reasons of this change are not clear[307], but the effects are: the original

---

[306] See p. 172, Teresa Scassa, *Language of judgment and the Supreme Court of Canada*, 43 U.N.B.L.J. (1994).

[307] Several explanations have been brought forward. One would be Justice Pigeon's passing: he was indeed an advocate of bilingualism and wanted the two versions of

version was to be considered the authoritative one[308]. This practice resulted in an overwhelming number of decisions reported in English with a French translation.

Although this was the main practice between 1980 and 1988, there were also some decisions whose report bore no indication of the drafting language. These

---

each judgment to be authoritative. Some justices might have thought that for purposes of interpretation it would have been easier to make clear which version was the authoritative one. Another explanation put forward by Teresa Scassa would be the growth of the translating facilities at the Supreme Court: translators taking pride in their work could have wished their participation to be mentioned. – See p. 172-173, Teresa Scassa, *Language of judgment and the Supreme Court of Canada*, 43 U.N.B.L.J. (1994).

[308] In theory both versions had equal value, but in practice in case of differences between the two versions, one would look for the justices' true intent. How could a mere translation be considered to epitomize a justice's opinion better than a text that s/he has written her/himself?

decisions were made either in cases from Quebec, cases on languages rights or cases of a constitutional nature[309]. Such deviations from the general practice (which were not systematic) seem to have been chosen either in order to respect the parties' language[310] or to adopt a linguistically neutral approach in some sensitive cases.

On the whole, during this period, all decisions were published in both languages but the authoritative versions of most of them were in English. The Court had *de facto* turned to an English-based bilingualism.

---

[309] See p. 174, Teresa Scassa, *Language of judgment and the Supreme Court of Canada*, 43 U.N.B.L.J. (1994).

[310] In cases where the two parties used different languages.

dd) 1988 – today: The second Official Languages Act

In 1988, the first *Official Languages Act* was replaced by a new one. Sections 14 to 20 of the new act gave a more detailed framework for language use in justice[311]. This act did not have much impact on the Court's practices. It could in fact be said that it codified its existing practices[312]. Since 1988, the Court's decisions have continued to be predominantly drafted in English and translated into French.

Decisions with no indications concerning the drafting language are also occasionally delivered. Like in the prior period, such decisions usually deal with controversial

---

[311] It was section 5 of the first *Official Languages Act* which dealt with language in the administration of justice.

[312] See p. 175, Teresa Scassa, *Language of judgment and the Supreme Court of Canada*, 43 U.N.B.L.J. (1994).

issues. Important decisions on issues of national character or language rights tend to be reported in a language neutral way.

Decisions concerning Quebec tend to be written in French and translated into English (especially when the parties are French-speakers).

Another development is the practice of Justice L'Heureux-Dubé whose decisions have been reported without any mention of the drafting language since 1992. This highly symbolic choice seems to echo Justice Pigeon's vision of a bilingual court whose decisions would be equally authoritative in both languages.

With the appointment of Louise Arbour in 1999, for the first time in the Court's history, a majority of the judges speak French.

Even so, the Court's linguistic center of gravity has remained English.

(2) The equal authenticity rule and its implications

Since English and French were both the official languages, and since (for political reasons detailed above) letting one language have precedence over the other one was (and is) out of the question, the justices had to admit that the two versions of the law had (at least in theory) the same authority. This principle is enshrined in the *Canadian Charter of Rights and Freedoms*[313] and in the *Official Languages Act*[314]. The equal authenticity rule

---

[313] Section 16: *"English and French are the official languages of Canada and have equality of status…"*.

[314] Section 2 a): *"The purpose of this act is to ensure respect for English and French as the official languages of Canada*

applies to statutes but also to court judgments[315].

This principle brought along its share of problems. In case of ambiguity or difference between the two versions of a statute or a judgment, Courts need to establish its true meaning. This can be an open door to arbitrary or inaccurate interpretations.

Faced with this difficulty, the Supreme Court came up with its own way of interpreting the law. In the words of justice L'Heureux-Dubé: *"Interpretation (...) necessitates reading the two texts in light of one another"*[316].

---

and ensure equality of status (...) in the administration of justice..." and Section 14: *"English and French are the official languages of the federal courts..."*.

[315] Indeed, as provided by section 20 of the *Official Languages Act*, any final decision, order or judgment issued by any federal court shall be made available in both official languages.

[316] See p. 452, Claire l'Heureux Dubé, *Bijuralism : A Supreme*

This method of interpretation seems to be the only way to respect legal bilingualism (and the equal authority of each version of the law). If this method was not used, the very principle of legal bilingualism would be at risk[317].

Yet, this method can only be used by someone bilingual. Not all Canadian judges have a good command of the two official languages and the vast majority of Canadian

---

Court of Canada Justice's perspective, 62 La. L. Rev. 451 (2001-2002)

[317] "Legal bilingualism presupposes finding a method for reading and interpreting these legal materials that recognizes their equal authority... and that, in Canada, necessarily draws on both English- and French- language versions. Without such a methodology, the promise of legal bilingualism risks being transformed into a practice of de facto legal dualism, that is, the pretence that Canadian law can be completely understood by referring to only one of the two official texts.", See p. 128-129, Roderick A. MacDonald, *Legal Bilingualism*, 42 McGill L.J. 119, 160-61 (1997)

citizens only speak English. If it is necessary to speak both languages in order to understand the true meaning of the law, then most Canadians cannot understand it. All they can do is read a text in their language and – if they need to rely on it – hope that the judges will not choose – in light of the other version – an interpretation which is different from the one they could have legitimately expected.

The knowledge of one of the official languages being insufficient for the purpose of understanding the law, one could argue that Canadian law exists neither in English or French but only in *Frenglish*.

(3) The method of interpretation of statutes

The problems linked to the equal authority rule are not theoretical. Cases based on purely semantic considerations are numerous. Supreme Court's method of interpretation was formed progressively, on a case-by-case basis.

aa) Interpreting each version of a statute in the light of the other

In the 1935 case *The King v. Dubois*, the Supreme Court on a petition of right claiming damages for the death of a passenger in a government automobile had to decide whether this automobile was a *"public work"* in the sense of section 19(c) of the *Exchequer Court Act*.

The Exchequer Court had decided that the automobile was a *"public work"* but the

Supreme Court reversed this judgement after considering the French version of the Act in which the terms used in place of *"public work"* were *"chantier public"* (*"chantier"* means *"building site"*). Basing its decision on these linguistic considerations, the Supreme Court decided that *"chantier"* (and therefore *"public work"*) referred to a defined area, a locality and could not include a government vehicle. The English version of the Act was interpreted in the light of the French version.

Regardless of how logical the Supreme Court's decision was, it is troubling to think that the meaning of the *Exchequer Court Act* was not understood by the judges of the Exchequer Court.

The Supreme Court followed and still follows this precedent[318] but also works not to

---

[318] In a similar case (*R. v. Moscovitz*) decided shortly after,

let subtle linguistic differences be resorted to at the expense of the legislators' intent.

In *Davis v. The City of Montreal*, a former Superintendent of Water-works argued that his dismissal by resolution of the city council was wrongful. On appeal at the Supreme Court, he compared the English and French versions of the city statute which empowered the city council to employ persons to work for it. The text stated that the city council *"may (...) at its pleasure remove any such officer and appoint another in his place"*. Davis argued that the French version of the text, where *"at its pleasure"* was phrased *"à sa discretion"*, meant something different and that it his dismissal by the council was thus wrongful. The court ruled that even though there might be a slight difference between the English and the

---

the Court followed the *Dubois* precedent.

French expressions, both versions clearly indicated the legislator's intention to give arbitrary powers to the city council in the field of human resources[319].

bb) Looking into the genesis of each piece of legislation

In cases were phrasing in the two languages clearly opens two distinct interpretations, courts need to make a choice. The Supreme Court's solution for dealing with such situations was to look into the genesis of each piece of legislation in order to find the idea(s) that the legislator intended to express.

---

[319] See p. 149, Claude-Armand Sheppard, *The Law of Languages in Canada*, Studies of the Royal Commission on Bilingualism and Biculturalism, Information Canada (Ottawa, 1971).

The Supreme Court was for instance called to interpret the meaning of the words *"personal wrongs"* in article 421 of the former *Quebec Code of Procedure*[320]. This article gave the right to a trial by jury *"in all actions for the recovery of damages resulting from personal wrongs"*. In the French version, the idea of *"personal wrongs"* was expressed by the terms *"torts personnels"*. Mr. Justice Brodeur admitted that the meaning of the expression *"torts personnels"* eluded him but he noted that it had originated in a literal translation from a 1785 English statute in which the words *"personal wrongs"* first appeared. He also noted that trial by jury in civil cases was a practice borrowed from English law. The Court's view was therefore that the interpretation of the words *"torts personnels"*

---

[320] Now article 332.

should be made on the basis of the English version of the law[321].

Similarly when a text of law which is not clear is based upon, or consolidates, earlier laws, the Court will consult them and use them to interpret the meaning of the law[322].

cc) Protecting the interests of the people

---

[321] See p. 149, Claude-Armand Sheppard, *The Law of Languages in Canada*, Studies of the Royal Commission on Bilingualism and Biculturalism, Information Canada (Ottawa, 1971).

[322] See p. 151, Claude-Armand Sheppard, *The Law of Languages in Canada*, Studies of the Royal Commission on Bilingualism and Biculturalism, Information Canada (Ottawa, 1971).

Where one version of a statute is inaccurate, doubtful or ambiguous while the other version is clear, the clear version is applied. But where the two versions are clearly contradictory they nullify each other[323].

In criminal matters, the rule adopted by the Supreme Court is that when two interpretations of a statute are possible, the interpretation which is the most favourable to the accused will prevail[324].

(4) Interpretation of two versions of a court judgment

---

[323] See p. 151, Claude-Armand Sheppard, *The Law of Languages in Canada*, Studies of the Royal Commission on Bilingualism and Biculturalism, Information Canada (Ottawa, 1971).

[324] See p. 151, Claude-Armand Sheppard, *The Law of Languages in Canada*, Studies of the Royal Commission on Bilingualism and Biculturalism, Information Canada (Ottawa, 1971).

Two versions of a judgment can differ and pose the same problems as two diverging versions of a piece of legislation. Determining the meaning of a decision can in some cases be quite arduous, arguably even more than determining the meaning of a statute[325].

---

[325] Indeed, statutes are usually shorter and clearer while court decisions can sometimes be quite lengthy and literary. – *"It is part of the normal task of a court to interpret the meaning of statutes. Thus, regardless of the degree of divergence between the different language texts, these differences will always be resolvable by judicial interpretation. Judgments, on the other hand, form a strange hybrid between the legal and the literary. On the one hand, they are designed to have a binding legal effect, yet on the other hand they are texts which can express the values, thought processes and personal styles of their authors. Judgments are not written in a way which is amenable to the 'simultaneous' drafting process which has revolutionized the preparation of multilingual statutes. They present the usual problems of legal translation in that they are meant to interpret the law, and yet, through divergences in meaning across language, they are themselves often capable of multiple interpretations"* See p. 180, Teresa

While the *Official Languages Act* provides for the bilingualism of decisions issued by federal courts, it does not contain any guidelines regarding their interpretation.

The *Supreme Court Act* and the *Rules of the Supreme Court of Canada*[326] are silent concerning the language of judgment. The rules of the Court do not provide for the drafting of the original text of a judgment in a particular language (judges as well as parties use the official language they want[327]), nor do they explain how the Court should deal with the question of the authoritativeness of the two versions of a judgment. Obviously, the original version of a judgment retains an advantage on the translated version. Differences between the two versions are

---

Scassa, *Language of judgment and the Supreme Court of Canada*, 43 U.N.B.L.J. (1994).

[326] SOR/83-74

[327] See above II, D, 3, b), (1): Language(s) of work

more likely to be blamed on the translator than on the drafter. Poor translations render the equal authenticity rule inapplicable. In such cases, the two versions of a judgment will not be considered equally authoritative and the original version will be used as a reference. The mention of the drafting language (or its absence) on a judgment can therefore have big implications for its interpretation.

Indeed, in the absence of clear rules of interpretation, the Court deals with judgments the way it deals with statutes, interpreting one version in the light of the other and looking into the meaning of the judgment.

CONCLUSION

It seems that the Canadian official bilingualism has not created a system where English and French are the official languages but where English and French combined are the official language[328]. To read the bilingual menu of the restaurant[329], patrons need to

---

[328] *"Just as drafters of bilingual legislation are engaged in the translation of a single juridical idea into two natural languages, interpreters would come to accept that knowledge of one version alone is an insufficient point of reference for understanding the idea in question. They would understand legislative texts as fully embracing both English and French connotations and contexts, and as necessarily meaning what both versions say. No longer would it be possible to speak of two texts being equally authoritative. To the extent that any formulation of a legal rule can be authoritative, it will be necessary to speak of one authoritative bilingual text in French and English."*, Roderick A. MacDonald, *Legal Bilingualism*, 42 McGill L.J. 119, 160-61 (1997)

master the two languages otherwise they might end up getting something different from what they thought they ordered: a *deep apple pie* instead of a *pie with deep apples* for example.

The principle of equality between the languages being an expression of the equality of all Canadian citizens could hardly be presented as an unfair concept. Yet its paradoxical outcome is that equality can only be fulfilled by bilingualism... and bilingualism means that all of those who are not bilingual do not have access to the law.

Canada's way of dealing with the coexistence and cooperation of two cultures has its flaws, disadvantages and paradoxes. One could argue that this approach to

---

[329] Cf. F.R. Scott's poem presented on page 2 of the dissertation.

bilingualism damages to the preciseness of the law. Legal words are tools that need to be sharp.

But in our globalized world, cultures meet and legal systems blend. Virtually all regional and global institutions created since the 20th century (be it the U.N., the E.U. or even the F.I.F.A.[330]) have had to face the challenge of producing multilingual rules that can be acceptable and workable for all of their members. Law faces new cultural and linguistic challenges every day.

From this perspective, the Canadian experience can be seen as an interesting and inspiring example of legislation and administration of justice in a truly multicultural society.

---

[330] Fédération Internationale de Football Association (international governing body of football).

BIBLIOGRAPHY

Nota : *Apart from the quotes by Blaise Pascal or Alexis de Tocqueville, the French sources were translated into English by the author.*

Reference books

Anderson G.W. (Ed.), *Rights and Democracy: Essays in UK-Canadian constitutionalism*, Blackstone (London, 1999)

Bouchard G. and Lacombe M., *Dialogue sur les pays neufs*, Boréal (1999)

Bourthillier G. and Meynaud J., *Le Choc des langues au Québec*, Les Presses de l'Université du Québec (1972)

Brunet M., *Out of the Shadows: The Civil Law Tradition in the Department of Justice Canada*, Department of Justice Canada (Ottawa, 2000)

Cardin J.F. & Couture C., *Histoire du Canada, Espaces et différences*, Les Presses de l'Université de Laval

Careless J.M.S., *Canada, a story of challenge*, MacMillan (1963)

Champagne A., *L'histoire du régime français*, Editions Septentrion (Sillery, Québec, 1996)

Creighton D., *Canada's first century*, MacMillan (Toronto, 1970).

Creighton D., *Dominion of the North*, MacMillan, 2nd edition (Toronto, 1966)

Garneau F.X., *Histoire du Canada*, 1860

Glenn H. P., *Droit Québécois et Droit Français: Communauté, Autonomie, Concordance*, Ed° Yvon Blais Inc. (Cowansville, Québec, 1993)

Glenn H. P., *Legal Traditions of the World*, O.U.P. (2000)

Harlow C. and Rawlings R., *Pressure Through Law*, Routledge, 1992

Havard G. and Vidal C., *Histoire de l'Amérique Française*, Flammarion (Paris, 2003)

Jacob H., Blankenburg E., Kritzer H.M., Provine D.M., Sanders J., *Courts, Law, and Politics in Comparative Perspective*, Yale University Press (1996)

Katz A.N., *Legal traditions and systems*, Greenwood Press (Westport, United States of America, 1986)

Legrand P. and Munday R., *Comparative legal studies: Traditions and Transitions*, Cambridge University Press (2003)

McNaught K., *The Pelican History of Canada*, Penguin Books, 2nd edition (London, 1978)

Mélanges Louis-Philippe Pigeon, Wilson & Lafleur (Montreal, 1989)

Merryman J. H., *The Loneliness of the Comparative Lawyer*, Kluwer Law International (1999)

Orücü E., *Studies in Legal Systems: "Mixed and Mixing"*, Kluwer Law International (1996)

Patterson D.G., *Nunavut Legal Services Study: Final Report*, Department of Justice Canada (Ottawa, 2004)

Robinson O.F., Fergus T.D., Gordon W.M., *European Legal History*, 3rd Edition, Butterworths (2000)

Russell P., *The Supreme Court of Canada as a Bilingual and Bicultural Institution*, Studies of the Royal Commission on Bilingualism and Biculturalism, Information Canada (Ottawa, 1969)

Schmid C., *The Politics of Language*, Oxford University Press ???

Sheppard C.A., *The Law of Languages in Canada*, Studies of the Royal Commission on Bilingualism and Biculturalism, Information Canada (Ottawa, 1971)

Zweigert K. and Kötz H., *An Introduction to Comparative Law*, O.U.P. (1998)

Articles

De Broglie G., *La Langue du Code Civil*, Académie des Sciences Morales et Politiques (Paris) ???

Iacobucci F., *The Supreme Court of Canada: its history, powers and responsibilities*, 4 J. App. Prac. & Process 39 (2002)

Kasirer N., *Dire ou définir le droit?*, 28 R.J.T. n.s., 1994

MacDonald R. A., *"Encoding Canadian Civil Law"* in *"The Harmonization of Federal Legislation with Quebec Civil Law and Canadian Bijuralism: Collection of Studies"*, Department of Justice Canada (Ottawa, 1997)

MacDonald R.A., *Legal Bilingualism*, 42 McGill L.J. 119 (1997)

McLachlin B., *Aboriginal Peoples and Reconciliation*, 9 Canterbury L. Rev. (2003)

Revell D.L., *Authoring bilingual laws: the importance of process*, Brook. J. Int'l. L. Vol. 29:3 2004, pp. 1085-1105

Revell D.L., *Bilingual Legislation: The Ontario Experience*, Statute Law Review, Volume 19, Number 1, pp. 32-40, 1998

Russell P.H., *Introduction: History and Development of the Court in National Society - The Canadian Supreme Court*, 3 Can. – U.S. L.J. (1980).

Scassa T., *Language of judgment and the Supreme Court of Canada*, 43 U.N.B.L.J. (1994).

Stonet A.N., *Bilingual drafting in a Common law jurisdiction in Canada*, Statute Law Review, 1987.

Websites

Aboriginals

The Indigenous Bar Association:

    www.indigenousbar.ca

The Aboriginal Mapping Network:

    www.nativemaps.com

Americana / Canadiana

Alexis de Tocqueville in America:

    www.tocqueville.org

Canada in the Making

    www.canadiana.org

Bilingualism

Commissioner of Official Languages

    www.ocol-clo.gc.ca

Federal Translation Bureau

    www.translationbureau.gc.ca

History of official bilingualism

    www.mapleleafweb.com

Canadian Provinces

Ministry of Justice of Nunavut:

    www.justice.gov.nu.ca

Office Québécois de la Langue Française:

    www.oqlf.gouv.qc.ca

Canadian Law

Canadian Legal Information Institute:

    www.canlii.org

Federal institutions

Department of Justice Canada
    http://canada.justice.gc.ca
Parliament of Canada
    www.parl.gc.ca

Miscellaneous

Canada, Confederation to Present, An interactive history of Canada, CD-Rom, Chinook Publications (Edmonton, Alberta), 2001

Emerson R.W., *The American Scholar*, lecture delivered before the Phi Beta Kappa society in Harvard, 1837

Hutchinson W., *La question irlandaise*, Ellipses (Paris, 2001)

Kalm P., *Travels in North America*, 1770

Microsoft Encarta Reference Library, 2004

Montesquieu, *De l'Esprit des Lois*, 1748

Ohmae K., *Triad Power, the coming shape of global competition*, Free Press, 1985, 220 p.

Pascal Blaise, *Pensées*, Gallimard, 1995 (first published in 1669), 764 p.

Publius, *The Federalist*

Scott F.R., *The Blasted Pine,* Macmillan (Toronto), 1957, 138 p.

Titus Livius, *History of Rome (Ab Urbe Condita)*

Tocqueville A., *Journey to America*, Greenwood Press Publishers, Westport, C.T., 1981

Vesilund P.J., *Common Ground, Different Dreams*, National Geographic, February 2000.

ANNEXES

Chart 1 – Population by Ethnic Origin (1871)

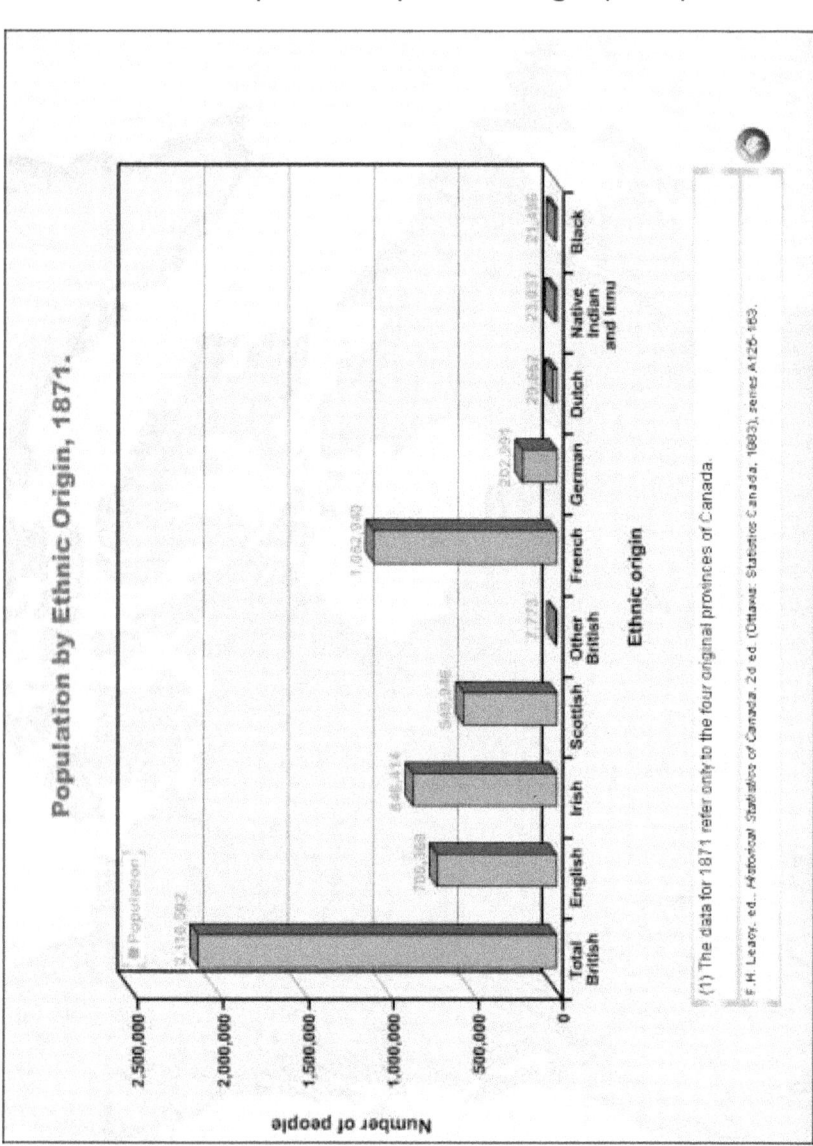

Source: *Canada, Confederation to Present, An interactive history of Canada*, CD-Rom, Chinook Publications (Edmonton, Alberta), 2001

Chart 2 – Population by Mother Tongues (1867)

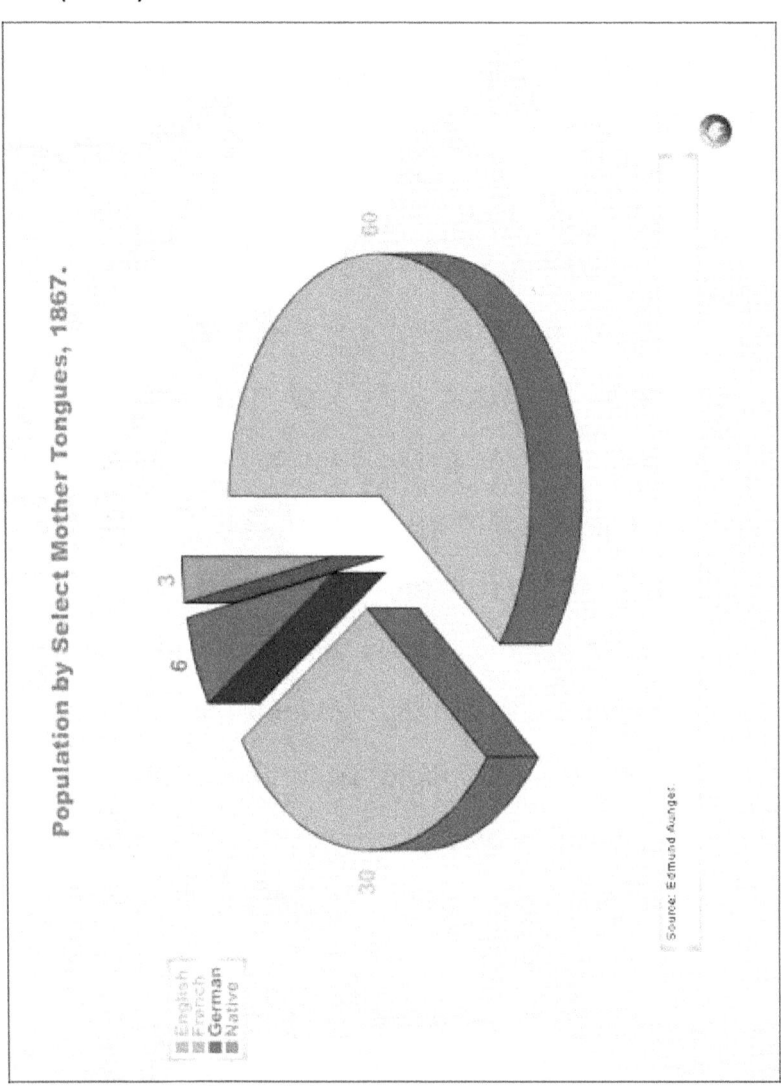

Source: *Canada, Confederation to Present, An interactive history of Canada*, CD-Rom, Chinook Publications (Edmonton, Alberta), 2001

Text 1 – A traveller's view of the French Canadians

Excerpt from *Travels in North America* by Peter Kalm (1770)

"The difference between the manners and customs of the French in Montreal and Canada, and those of the English in the American colonies, is as great as that between the manners of those two nations in Europe. The women in general are handsome here; they are well bred and virtuous, with an innocent and becoming freedom. They dress up very fine on Sundays; about the same as our Swedish women, and though on the other days they do not take much pains with other parts of their dress, yet they are very fond of adorning their heads. Their hair is always curled, powdered and ornamented with glittering bodkins [ornamental hairpins] and

aigrettes [clusters of gems]. Every day but Sunday they wear a little neat jacket, and a short skirt which hardly reaches halfway down the leg, and sometimes not that far. And in this particular they seem to imitate the Indian women. The heels of their shoes are high and very narrow, and it is surprising how they can walk on them. In their domestic duties they greatly surpass the English women in the plantations, who indeed have taken the liberty of throwing all the burden of housekeeping upon their husbands, and sit in their chairs all day with folded arms. The women in Canada on the contrary do not spare themselves, especially among the common people, where they are always in the fields, meadows, stables, etc. and do not dislike any work whatsoever. However, they seem rather remiss in regard to the cleaning of the utensils and apartments, for sometimes the floors, both in the town and country, are hardly cleaned once in six months, which is a disagreeable sight to one who comes from amongst the Dutch and English, where the constant scouring and scrubbing of the floors is reckoned as important as the exercise of religion itself. To prevent the thick dust, which is thus left on the floor from being noxious to the health, the women wet it several times a day, which lays the dust, and they repeat this as often as the dust is dry and begins to rise again. Upon the whole, however, they are not averse to the taking part in all the business of housekeeping, and I have with pleasure seen the daughters of the better sort of people and of the governor himself, not too finely dressed, going into kitchens and cellars to see that everything was done as it ought to be. And they also carry their sewing with them, even the governor's daughters.

The men are extremely civil and take their hats off to every person whom they meet in the streets. This is difficult for anyone whose duties demand that he be out doors often, especially in the evening when every family sits outside their door, near the street. It is customary to return a visit the day after you have received one, even though one should have several scores to pay in one day.

(...)

All the women in the country without exception, wear caps of some kind or other. Their jackets are short and so are their skirts, which scarcely reach down to the middle of their legs. Their shoes are often like those of the Finnish women, but are sometimes provided with heels. They have a silver cross hanging down on the breast. In general they are very industrious. However I saw some, who, like the English women in the colonies, did nothing but prattle all day. When they have anything to do within doors, they (especially the girls) commonly sing songs in which the words amour and coeur are very frequent. In the country it is usual that when the husband receives a visit from persons of rank and dines with them, his wife stands behind and serves him, but in the town the ladies are more distinguished, and would willingly assume an equal if not a superior position to their husbands. When they go out of doors they wear long cloaks, which cover all their other clothes and are either grey, brown or blue. Men sometimes make use of them when they are obliged to walk in the rain. The women have the advantage of being in a déshabillé [negligee] under these cloaks, without anybody's perceiving it.

(...)

The civility of the inhabitants here is more refined than that of the Dutch and English in the settlements belonging to Great Britain. On the street they raised their hat only to acquaintances and to those of the upper classes. Young men often kept their hats on inside where there were women, but most of them, especially the older ones, took them off. The English, on the other hand, do not idle their time away in dressing as the French do here. The ladies, especially, dress and powder their hair every day, and put their locks in papers every night. This idle custom had not been introduced in the English settlements. The gentlemen generally wear their own hair, but some have wigs, and there were a few so distinguished that they had a queue. People of rank are accustomed to wear lace-trimmed clothes and all the crown officers carry swords. All the gentlemen, even those of rank, the governor-general excepted, when they go into town on a day that looks like rain, carry their cloaks on their left arm. Acquaintances of either sex, who have not seen each other for some time, on meeting again salute with mutual kisses."

Text 2 – A trial in Quebec

Excerpt from *Journey to America* by Alexis de Tocqueville

"We came into a large hall divided into tiers crowded with people who seemed altogether French. The British arms were painted in full size on the end of the hall. Beneath them was the judge in robes and bands. The lawyers were ranked in front of him.

When we came into the hall a slander action was in progress. It was a question of fining a man who had called another pendard (gallows-bird) and crasseux (stinker). The lawyer argued in English. Pendard, he said, pronouncing the word with a thoroughly English accent, "meant a man who had been hanged." No, the judge solemnly intervened, but who ought to be. At that, counsel for the defense got up indignantly and argued his case in French: his adversary answered in English.

The argument waxed hot on both sides in English, no doubt without their understanding each other perfectly. From time to time the Englishman forced himself to put his argument in French so as to follow his adversary more closely; the other did the same sometimes. The judge, sometimes speaking French, sometimes English, endeavored to keep order. The crier of the court called for "silence" giving the word alternatively its English and its French pronunciation.

Calm re-established, witnesses were heard. Some kissed the silver Christ on the Bible and swore in French to tell the truth, the others swore the same oath in English and, as Protestants, kissed the other side of the Bible which was undecorated. The customs of Normandy were cited, reliance placed on Denisart, and mention was made of the decrees of the Parliament of Paris and statutes of the reign of George III. After that the judge: "Granted that the word crasseux implies that a man is without morality, ill-behaved and dishonorable, I order the defendant to pay a fine of ten louis or ten pounds sterling."

The lawyers I saw there, who are said to be the best in Quebec, gave no proof of talent either in the substance or in the manner of what they said. They were conspicuously lacking in distinction, speaking French with a middle class Norman accent. Their style is vulgar and mixed with odd idioms and English phrases. They say that a man is charge of ten louis meaning that he is asked to pay ten louis. "Entrez dans la boite"[331], they shout to a witness, meaning that he should take his place in the witness-box.

There is something odd, incoherent, even burlesque in the whole picture. But at the bottom the impression made was one of sadness. Never have I felt more convinced than when coming out from there, that the greatest and most irremediable ill for a people is to be conquered".

---

[331] Entrez dans la boîte means "Enter the box"

www.ingramcontent.com/pod-product-compliance
Lightning Source LLC
Chambersburg PA
CBHW051759170526
45167CB00005B/1803